AF413679

Advance Praise for *Lead With Kindness*

"There's no one I trust more to speak from experience on how to be a good leader in Hollywood—or anywhere. Melinda's advice is not just practical and thoughtful, it's inspirational. She is one of a kind—and she's worth listening to, in her book and on her podcast."

—Maureen "Mo" Ryan, TV critic, contributing editor at Vanity Fair, and author of *Burn It Down: Power, Complicity, and a Call for Change in Hollywood*

"If you are lucky enough to lead artists, then take my advice and sit at Melinda Hsu's feet (or crack open this book) immediately. Her sacred tenets: that one can lead with kindness, that creatives need safe environments to explore, and that humility—not the ability to instill fear—is her greatest strength, transformed me as a manager and can help create better workplaces for all those who hope to create and lead."

—Cameron Johnson, TV writer, producer, and creator of *Tom Swift*

LEAD
with
KINDNESS

LEAD

with

KINDNESS

How to Change the Culture of the Workplace and the World

MELINDA HSU

A POST HILL PRESS BOOK
ISBN: 979-8-89565-228-2
ISBN (eBook): 979-8-89565-229-9

Lead With Kindness:
How to Change the Culture of the Workplace and the World
© 2026 by Melinda Hsu
All Rights Reserved

Cover design by Jim Villaflores

This book, as well as any other Post Hill Press publications, may be purchased in bulk quantities at a special discounted rate. Contact orders@posthillpress.com for more information.

Post Hill Press
New York • Nashville
posthillpress.com

Published in the United States of America
1 2 3 4 5 6 7 8 9 10

*Dedicated to my mother, Dr. Martha Tih Hsu,
who modeled kindness with spectacular grace.*

TABLE OF CONTENTS

WHY WRITE A BOOK ABOUT KINDNESS?

A few days into the Writers Guild of America strike in May of 2023, I was startled to find myself experiencing fifteen minutes of fame due to my off-the-cuff interview about the issues at stake. In a concise burst of passion, I told a video journalist how studios had created pay structures where all writers received the same entry-level salary regardless of previous experience and why I felt it was reasonable that my work should be valued differently after twenty years on the job as a unionized TV writer. Ninety seconds, 2.5 million views on TikTok,[1] and a month later, I was still getting approached by strangers who had sent my picket-line interview to anyone who wanted a convincing distillation of why thousands of writers were marching the perimeters of the studios.

And then *Vanity Fair* published a scathing excerpt from Maureen Ryan's book *Burn It Down*—in which she exposed the harassment, discrimination, and aggressions that ran rampant in the writers' room at *Lost*—and I was one of the people who had

---

[1] Mike Gauyo (@blackboywrites), "This," May 5, 2023, https://x.com/blackboy
writes/status/1654521002234380288?s=20.

gone on the record about the dysfunctional leadership that had impacted me during my years on the writing staff of one of the world's most popular TV shows.

Once again, strangers started approaching me on the picket line. They told me about their own experiences with abusive leaders and brutal environments across a myriad of industries and asked me versions of the same question: "How do things get *so bad* in a workplace? What are the complex nuances that result in such a toxic situation?"

And I would always answer: "It isn't nuanced. It's not rocket science. If leaders had *once* told the team, 'We want you people to treat each other with kindness and professionalism. Show us you can do that. *That* will please us,' then we would have radically changed our behavior." I included myself in the "we," because on my way up the ranks I had often stayed quiet to survive in an industry riddled with workplaces that were unforgiving to women, unwelcoming to people of color, and soul-crushing for parents like me who were trying to navigate the simultaneous demands of career and child-raising.

But in these conversations on the picket line, I was also able to share how much my perspective and empowerment had evolved during twenty years of continuous employment as a TV writer. I was no longer a rank-and-file staff member. I had sold multiple pilots to networks and streaming platforms; I had been an executive producer, cocreator, and showrunner in charge of network TV series for years and had recently become an episodic director as well.

In all of those positions, instead of perpetuating the abuse I had endured, I had analyzed my past experiences and found ways to be a different sort of leader, one who created respectful, inclusive, humane workplaces where people's creativity flourished.

They gave 1000 percent, not because they were afraid of being fired or because they were trying to decimate colleagues—but because they wholeheartedly wanted to elevate the entire team, and because they felt securely and meaningfully connected to the collaboration at hand. (And for the record, I have only seen 1000-percent efforts from people who truly loved and trusted the human surroundings they were in. Fear and divisiveness can never elicit even 100 percent from your team, because part of their energy will always be siphoned off by looking over their shoulders and scanning for possible exits.)

Reflecting on my journey, I realized that because of those many years of gutting it out in the dysfunctional trenches, I had taught myself how to *lead with kindness.*

Not only that, but my success could be replicated: modeled, fostered, and instilled—just as I had done with the writing staffs and TV productions I steered. Moreover, my strategies apply to domains far beyond Hollywood—to anywhere humans interact with each other, in fact. I am certain that the world is longing for more kindness. I don't know anyone who wants to experience *less* kindness, less effectiveness, less meaning in their life.

But most people don't know where to begin to improve their situations. And most people don't have concrete, relatable, and *spreadable* tools to create more harmony, success, and positive impact in their business and personal lives. I emphasize "spreadable" because, above all, I want people to share these tactics with each other, so that we can change society one relationship at a time. (Yes, I am that ambitious.)

That's why I've written my first book: *Lead With Kindness.*

But what if you're an overworked businessperson who doesn't think that kindness is a worthy goal in and of itself? What if, to you, kindness sounds warm and gentle and therefore weak and so is not worth your time? Couple things. First, don't confuse being kind with being nice. Niceness is about appearances; kindness is about intention. Second, don't mistake kindness for weakness. In my experience, it takes considerably more backbone to be consistently kind no matter what the circumstance. Sometimes the kindest thing to do is to have a painful conversation, enforce rigorous accountability, make a labor-intensive pivot, or require a colleague to abandon their comfort zone.

Here's why kindness is really worth your time, Overworked Businessperson: Kindness will bring you success, preserve your resources, and make you money. In every chapter, I will highlight the nonaltruistic ends achieved by all my means, and I will show that *kindness is better for business in every situation*. Even if you don't care whether people feel good, every sane businessperson cares whether people are productive, whether they stay in their organization or leave for greener pastures, and whether they commit to their jobs with efficiency and perseverance.

And here's how I know kindness works. My intentionally kind leadership as a TV showrunner fostered an atmosphere of possibility, where everyone was encouraged to devote time to what mattered in their personal lives as well as their professional ones. Where people with intersectional identities were recruited, valued, retained, and celebrated. Where meetings started on time and ended on time. Where fundamental trust among team members emboldened them to voice ideas freely and without fear, and where those ideas were respectfully and constructively received and responded to. Where expectations and schedules were stated with transparency and regularity—and scrupulously adhered to. Where people could go to the restroom whenever they felt the need. These items are in no particular order. (In an anecdote from the staff of a very prestigious TV show, a friend told me that the writers only took restroom breaks when their showrunner did: "We pee when he pees.")

Sharply contrasting to the dysfunction and toxicity that often characterize TV productions, the culture I created at *Nancy Drew* and our spin-off *Tom Swift* was widely known and envied for its kindness and warmth. Everyone on the writing staff, on the crew, and in the cast felt that their contributions were genuinely sought after and welcomed. Our episodes came in on time and on budget, following a precise and reasonable writing and production schedule that hundreds of people were looped in on. And not coincidentally, my harmonious teams put shows on the air that were beloved by audience members and network executives alike. In other words, my kindness resulted in measurable and elevated creative and business dividends.

To illuminate how these concepts manifest in business and in life, I started the *Lead With Kindness* podcast so that I could host conversations to transform our culture—not just the culture of Hollywood but the culture of how we treat each other in the world.

Season one of the podcast (connect on Instagram @melindahsuLA and listen on Apple Podcasts and Spotify) examines what I consider to be the ten essential elements of humane and healthy leadership:

- *Inclusion* allows people to bring their whole selves to the process, greatly enhancing the end products and the joy in the work.
- *Kindness* builds connection around a shared goal, radically increasing a team's cohesion and performance.
- *Trust* prompts your team to venture forth their best ideas for deeper collaboration and more fruitful innovation.

- *Love* shows respect for and commitment to mutual interests at the highest possible level. It transforms how you and your team approach whatever business is at hand.
- *Calm* incentivizes your team to help your enterprise succeed, because they'll know they can thrive long term in your orbit.
- *Transparency* empowers your team to help you reach objectives—which allows you to gain strength *because* you've acted from humility.
- *Work-life integration* results in your team staying longer and contributing more effectively because their time is valued and their boundaries are respected.
- *Accountability* lets your team know they are seen, afforded dignity, and taken care of. This ensures a more profound commitment to your desired outcomes.
- *Safety* as an absolute priority (physical, mental, and emotional) makes it possible for your team to do their best work.
- *Service* to others gives your team a sense of purpose and a personal stake in something outside of themselves, which is the key to sustainable productivity.

During each thirty-minute episode (I was very disciplined about their length and the usefulness of their reflections, because when have you ever listened to a podcast and thought, "I wish that episode had rambled on for another fourteen minutes?"), my colleagues and collaborators, as well as a few outside experts, candidly discuss how to change work-and-life dynamics through deliberately fostering and modeling these ten attributes.

Springboarding from my podcast, my book provides a separate wealth of relatable guidance on these topics, in ten easily digestible chapters. With the same accessible straight talk that made me a TikTok favorite, I'll convey how leading with kindness is way better for your business and for your soul. You'll see these business practices through my unique lens on leadership as a woman, a person of color, a mother, and a daughter of immigrants who left China as refugees. And to optimize your time, at the end of every chapter, I'll provide executive highlights (a snack-sized takeaway, a business benefit, a sustainable strategy, and several pro tips on how to put these ideas into action, even if you're not the boss yet) for those of you who can't be bothered to read the whole chapter.

Though the testing ground for my philosophy has been in TV writers' rooms and production settings, the audience for this book is not limited to people who make and/or love TV shows. The book is meant for literally anyone who interacts with other humans. *These strategies work across all walks of life because they tap into deeply universal needs for respect, agency, and connection.* And, my advice goes step-by-step. In these pages, you'll learn how to:

- build trust through authentic connection,
- say *no* in a way that speeds you along to the results you want,
- inspire loyalty and increase motivation,
- maintain internal stability for yourself and others,
- hold team members accountable to you and vice versa,
- and so much more.

Whether you're a leader or a team member, my principles and tactics will prompt a quantum leap in effectiveness when you craft, engage in, and revolutionize group dynamics. On an organizational level, this book is for people who want to get better results, increase profits, and remedy dysfunction and toxicity.

On a personal level, applied correctly and sincerely, these principles will also result in heartfelt relationships, lasting bonds, and improved well-being.

I was compelled to write *Lead With Kindness* because whenever I meet someone, I'm determined to help them become the greatest version of themself. I'll bring that greatness out of them even if the other person doesn't see it. I hope when you read my book, you'll realize that I'm already seeing the greatest version of you, even if I've never met you. I want to inspire you to prioritize and manifest kindness in your own actions and foster that kindness in every person you encounter. I invite you to use kindness as a powerful fuel for transformation—in yourself, in those around you, and, ultimately, in the world.

And now, to discover how I brought out the greatest version of two hundred team members on my latest TV series and to see how that was the best business decision I ever made, read on....

CHAPTER 1

INCLUSION MAKES YOU STRONGER

"Don't ever mistake
Melinda's kindness for weakness.
She could eat us all for lunch."

T his is what a colleague of mine told the writers' room of *The Vampire Diaries*, back when I was a writer-producer on that show. (For the record, I agreed.)

I share this anecdote in case you were thinking that anyone who authors a book about *leading with kindness* must be exceedingly delicate, naïve, and/or unused to the realities of high-stakes work environments.

The opposite is true. As a twenty-year veteran of TV writing and production, and as a showrunner and creator in charge of broadcast network series, I have been consistently surviving and frequently thriving in a brutally competitive, unforgiving, and demanding industry. I have met nerve-racking deadlines, navigated toxic workplaces, and upheld my creative and personal principles in the face of corporate bloodlettings. When in production as a showrunner, I supervise hundreds of people and report to a multitude of high-powered producers and studio and network executives. It's an intense pace that I enjoy: constantly putting out fires, steering a very large business enterprise, shepherding the individual processes of writers, actors, and craftspeople who have artistic natures and needs of their own, and maintaining my own perspective and sense of self throughout.

Here's how robust my business boundaries are in the midst of all that: I recently spoke on a panel at the Writers Guild Showrunner Training Program, and in response to the question of how I keep myself from becoming too friendly with the people on my teams, I replied, "When I look at anyone I work with, one part of my mind is always remembering: I might have to fire this person someday." Not because I ever expect or want to fire anybody, but there may be circumstances beyond my control that require a parting of the ways.

All this to say, I may be warm, but I am not fuzzy.

Yet—here's the twist—at every step in my career, I have become kinder and considerably more intentional about leading with kindness. Partly because it's the right thing to do, and let's not lose sight of that. But also because leading with kindness is a really smart business decision. Kindness prompts higher achievements. Kindness cultivates greater success. Kindness can and will work for *you.*

That last bit might get an eyebrow raise from the more skeptical people out there, and it's to those folks that I extend this assurance: You can read this entire book with a completely jaded, mercenary filter and still get a ton of useful insights to put into self-serving action. This book might warm your cold and calculating heart if you let it, but its main purpose is not to hand out hugs and gold stars. Instead, it provides *concrete guidelines to elevate your business results.*

In the course of delineating those guidelines, I will sometimes direct my comments to a hypothetical Overworked Businessperson who is unsure about the efficacy of adding kindness to their daily interactions. Please know that my wry debates with the Overworked Businessperson will be coming from a place of affection and understanding. All my asides are meant to answer the natural questions that emerge when considering radical paradigm shifts. They're also an invitation to pause for reflection amid all-consuming work lives where expediency has turned into habit, habit has become autopilot, and autopilot has devolved into unproductive or even harmful workplace culture.

I didn't have to write this book. I truly enjoy making a living as a TV writer-producer, I have a personal life that genuinely fulfills me, and the combination of the above keeps me quite busy. But, I decided to set aside a significant chunk of time for this endeavor because I think it's really important to spread these ideas around. So, I appreciate you considering my advice, because I know you can positively transform your professional life through intentionally and mindfully leading with kindness. Bonus: The planet will be a better place if we are all kinder to each other. (I never said I wasn't earnest.)

Spoiler for my thesis on leadership: *If you look people in the eye, acknowledge what they do, and treat their time as valuable, you will see marked and sustainable improvements in performance and outcomes.* Other benefits that may accrue from leading with kindness include but are not limited to increased sense of calm and well-being, willingness to see the best in others, ability to bring out the best in yourself, heightened skills to manage conflict and stress, and feeling that you're intentionally making the world even an incrementally better place.

That feeling gives this book added urgency, considering where the world is at the moment. As humans who share that world, it's absolutely doable to be kinder to each other; and as leaders who seek measurable success, it's imperative.

People have often asked me how I kept the production of *Nancy Drew* running on time and on budget, with satisfying and well-made episodes that TV audiences and network executives loved, and I always say it was very simple: I included my writers' ideas. Meaning: I kept as much of my staff's input and writing intact as possible, rather than constantly changing course on the storylines and unraveling scripts as we went along.

The latter two pitfalls frequently occur on TV shows, and analogous problems happen elsewhere in the work world too. There are so many nonentertainment places where people are told to complete a task and then their contributions are ignored, belittled, or undone by their supervisors; inevitably, morale suffers, and so do the end products.

With that in mind, let's stay above the canopy for a minute longer and address *the myth that harsh leadership is necessary to achieve results.* I came up the ranks in some very dysfunctional environments, and it still frustrates me to hear leaders in any field talk about their own foibles and inefficiency and disrespect for those around them as if these poor choices were a necessary part of striving for success. I firmly believe that these leaders don't realize that if they put all that energy toward being kind and inclusive instead of the opposite, they would solve the problems that they only *think* can be addressed via behaving like a moody, controlling, bias-governed narcissist.

But this is a book about kindness! On the topic of how great results happen because of—not in spite of—kind and inclusive leadership, let's drill down. First, I'll provide context on how I developed my own perspective on inclusion.

I grew up in the tiny town of Bangor, Maine. My parents were immigrants from China who were professors at the University of Maine, which is how our family ended up in a state where, at the time, about 99 percent of the population identified as White. I was timid and isolated as a kid and extremely self-conscious because I didn't look like anyone around me. So, I spent my childhood hiding in my bedroom, reading *The Lord of the Rings* over and over again and obsessing about *Star Wars* and *Star Trek*, because in all those stories if you were different, it was *cool*.

As an eight-year-old, sitting in my bedroom writing *Star Trek* fan fiction as a way to search for a sense of belonging in the world, I didn't realize that I was driven by the same unfulfilled needs that lie at the root of many dysfunctional workplaces. But now that I've observed and risen through severely othering environments to become an intentionally inclusive leader, I've learned how to bridge the divide between people who long to be seen and the established system they find themselves in. *Business benefit: the incredible output* that comes from acknowledging team members and sourcing participation from a wide range of identities.

**_Inclusion is an expansion and
empowerment of the team, a broadening
of viewpoints from perspectives and
experiences and backgrounds that
are not identical to your own._**

If you're in the position of assembling a team from scratch, congratulations! You can be extremely purposeful about finding people with many kinds of lived experiences; you can prioritize hiring people who are very different from each other in order to put together a staff that includes a range of ethnicities, genders, identities, physical abilities, ages, you name it. In recruiting multiple teams for my TV shows, I have found over and over again that an energetically inclusive hiring strategy makes the work better and the culture more uplifting.

However, if you're on an existing team with no need or budget for additional hires, I'm not mad at you, and these principles still entirely apply to your workplace. _Inclusion is a strategic operating style to maximize success._ If your team is already in place, I suggest you get curious about the people you work with. Ask for their opinions and find out what life experiences they've had that relate to the work you do together. You can also seek out training programs and consultants who specialize in identifying and overcoming unconscious bias. Additional sensitivities and frames of reference can only help your final products become more dimensional, relevant, and lasting.

Put another way: Including contributions is just as important as including people. It makes only a limited difference if you hire team members with a variety of lived experiences but then don't listen to their ideas, make them feel welcome, or sustain an environment where they can deepen their skills and get promoted. True inclusion incorporates all of the above.

Case Study: The TV Director

Here's a practical example of how to lead in an inclusive way. When veteran director Ruben Garcia arrives on set to film a scene of a television show, he thoughtfully communicates to everyone (the actors, plus the filming crew, plus the writers and producers) what his larger plan is and what his overall goals are. Instead of telling someone to stick the camera in a certain corner and telling the actors to stand in the opposite corner and say their lines, he shares his hope for what the audience will experience in the finished TV episode.

For instance, I heard him tell the crew on set, "We're entering this huge, creepy space that no one has ever been in before on *Nancy Drew*, so we're gonna start with a big, wide shot from the second-floor balcony to see our six heroes entering the hallway together. We won't even really see faces in that opening master shot. But then we'll bring the camera to floor level, and we'll start to do tighter shots to show the group in the frame, and then we'll go even closer to focus on a few people two by two, because those pairings have to relate to each other in this scene. And then for our last shot, we're just looking at Nancy's face when she opens that gate to go into the secret passage."

So, not just the actors but also the entire crew know where they fit into the team's unified goal of giving the audience a mysterious and wondrous entry into a haunted castle. The actors also know specifically when they will be called upon for emotional nuances in their close-ups. In this way, everyone is inspired to join forces as a single team—from the special-effects technicians pumping in dry ice to generate an eerie mist in this cavernous hallway that the art department designed and the construction department built, to the dolly grip who pushes the camera forward on its wheeled cart with the operator sitting astride it, to our actress Kennedy McMann as Nancy Drew herself, bringing the pivotal moment home.

You can use the Ruben Garcia method in any situation. When I was an assistant in the nutrition office of an AIDS service organization called God's Love We Deliver, one of my duties was to call nonprofits all over New York City and ask if they would like to have one of our nutritionists come out to give a free workshop for their clients living with HIV. Part of why I found this work meaningful, of course, was that people who were seropositive with limited resources would get the benefit of high-level nutritional counseling to help them manage their health. And fortunately, I worked for someone who wanted to connect me to the executive-level goals of what I was doing. These nutritional counseling visits were tracked by zip code and the demographics of the people served; that information was relayed to our grant manager, who reported nutritionists' activities to the government bodies that provided money to fund our department. By showing the metrics of what we were accomplishing in the field, we justified the continuation and renewal of these essential operating grants.

Because I had been included in the leadership's goals and thinking, I didn't feel like a cog who was making cold calls to people I would never meet. Instead, I felt I was a necessary piece of the puzzle in how all of us fulfilled our mission, which was to support people living with HIV in the five boroughs of New York and Hudson County, New Jersey.

Having been included in the big picture, I knew that when I scheduled a nutritional outreach, my task completion would keep our grant reporting on track and therefore allow money to flow in service of the many people who very much needed our help. Since I understood that our metrics (zip codes) supported a larger purpose (government grant money to keep the lights on), and because I knew how my individual actions made an impact, I got *so* good at booking those outreach presentations all over New York City and its surroundings. I assiduously packaged multilingual nutritional literature and carefully shipped box after box of pamphlets to all sorts of zip codes because I knew how each box helped the entire organization stay in the black and qualify for bigger grants to help even more people in the future.

So, quick regroup on inclusion strategies:

1. You value people's lived experiences in selecting and/or educating a team.
2. You welcome everyone's contributions.
3. You give context for how their individual efforts tie into your collective goals.

Doable, right? Yes. And to foster all of this and make it sustainable, it's incredibly important to build an environment where there is enough calm and enough time for ideas to be voiced, considered, adjusted, and then incorporated. Later chapters will cover how to create intentional calm and the many benefits of effective time management; all the topics in this book are interrelated and feed into each other. For now, remember that *actively valuing people's differing perspectives will greatly raise the caliber of the team's achievements.*

With that knowledge, you can look at your current leadership practices through the lens of these questions: Am I making it easier to include the thoughts of others? Or am I willfully denying their input? Or, through my own lack of planning and reluctance to make uncomfortable decisions, am I causing a bottleneck where no one has sufficient information or time to meet my (perhaps unstated or nebulous) needs and requests?

These are merely hypothetical questions, of course, and are only posed as an invitation to consider what adjustments you could possibly make in order to get better outcomes at work. (If you don't want better outcomes at work, you can put this book down right now. Just kidding. Please keep reading, and let me show you how completely accessible all of this is.)

In my capacity as a showrunner, I'm tasked with interviewing and hiring new writers for our staff. I recently interviewed a writer for a highly competitive position, and he impressed me by saying that he asks potential collaborators, "How do you like to be challenged?"

I love this question. It gets to the heart of what is wonderful and additive about inclusion. It's asking yourself and the team how they want their thoughts, expectations, and solutions to be enriched by soliciting the ideas of people who come from a variety of viewpoints.

Because when I use the word "challenge," I don't mean confrontation or defiance or negation. I mean an eye-opening perspective shift that leads to success—the kind of success that comes from sustainable innovation, educated negotiation, and a continual evolution of the work process itself.

I'm not saying you should accept challenging ideas, or any ideas, without vetting them rigorously. You should absolutely give feedback and ask for adjustments as needed. But, if you use *none* of the ideas you receive from your team, you should take a look at how clearly you're asking for what you want, because I'm willing to bet your communication specifics, or lack thereof, and possibly the manner in which you convey them, are negatively affecting the output from your team.

This doesn't mean you have to engage with every idea that is volunteered either. However, it's crucial to *acknowledge the fact* that an idea was offered, or that an email was sent to you. Even replying with "Received" is a million times better than having someone send an email into a void where you don't answer because you're unsure of what to say, you don't want to disappoint them, or (worse) you think you're too busy to be bothered with basic courtesy.

(A quick note on my use of the pronouns "they" and "them"—this is a choice on my part to make my advice and examples gender inclusive, and in some cases to obscure the clue trail as to which former colleague I might be referencing in an anecdote from my professional life. My choice won't always be grammatically correct by some standards, but I'm okay with that.)

Guess what? When you don't even acknowledge that people have done a task for you and made contact with you, your unresponsiveness has an extremely debilitating psychological impact. At best, your team will become discouraged and apathetic—because why try, if no one notices? At worst, they will become angry and mutinous—because why support a leader if your support is met with callous indifference?

If you think it's not important to acknowledge people's work, here are some examples of toxic unresponsiveness:

- A lead actor on a TV show sends a thoughtfully crafted and lengthy email to the showrunner, respectfully expressing concerns about their character and asking reasonable questions about where the season's storylines are headed. They get no response at all.

- At a public service organization that teaches job skills to adult refugees, staff members are expected to stay at the office well into the evening hours for no extra pay and to sacrifice weekends at the whim of the leader who founded the nonprofit. No mention is ever made of the fact that people's boundaries and time are not being respected.
- An organization hires a team dominated by White, straight men. The leader of the team separates the staff into two groups—one where people of color and women are doing busywork, and one where the leader and the other White, straight men are having substantive discussions and making decisions on action plans. No explanation is given for this division of team members.

Did all of these unacknowledged situations lead to plummeting morale and decreased accomplishments? Yes. And while some of the underlying issues in the examples above were much larger than a single unanswered email, the dynamic in all three is the same: People were not being acknowledged for the realities of their work.

⊕

But let's start small with this principle. Acknowledging the receipt of an email is a low and extremely achievable bar for leadership. A significant step above that is that you also *tell the sender exactly when you're going to get back to them about whatever they wrote.*

If you just had a knee-jerk reaction of "I can't possibly do that for every email! I'm way too busy and important for that! I'll get back to them when I get back to them, because their job is to wait for me!" then what you feel is very human. But, if you've been letting your feelings dictate your business tactics, then I'm guessing you are also being chased by the feeling that things are supposed to be going more smoothly, people around you are somehow letting you down despite how hard you're trying, and there's never enough time to get things done.

Deep breath: Here's a game changer for all of the above.

This is a tool pioneered by executive coach Birgit Zacher Hanson: *Who will do what by when, and why?* I'll expound on her principles of commitment management in chapter 8 on account-ability, but the nutshell is: Get agreement on next steps for the issue at hand. The next step might be as quick and final as thanking your colleague for their email, in which case your communication loop is complete. But if someone has emailed you with a request or a suggestion, that becomes a way to include them in your leadership process, which will build trust with them and then get them to work harder to generate more profits for you. (I haven't forgotten you, Overworked Businesspeople.)

A rudimentary example: Your subordinate emails you on Monday to ask if they can have fifteen minutes of your time for an in-person conversation. You might not know when your schedule will open up, but instead of leaving the email unanswered, you can at least reply with, "By Wednesday, I'll email you an answer about whether I have 15 minutes for you."

It might not be what they want to hear, but at least you haven't left them hanging, and at least they have a time (Wednesday) when they can expect to have your answer *about* the answer. The end result is that instead of feeling ignored, they feel included and acknowledged for their communication—and that makes all the difference in how they continue to commit and contribute.

And, the immediate benefit to you is that those energy drains—which happen when you know people are waiting for you to respond to their email/request/text/phone call/conversation—aren't being felt anymore, because you have acted as a responsible businessperson by not letting communications drift away into the ether. You are keeping your side of the street clean *by acknowledging that a team member asked you a question and by giving them a timeline for your response.*

This baseline respect and clarity towards your teammates is a shortcut to stability in your working dynamics. Increased stability means that you sleep better at night and get more done during the day. You're welcome!

An even higher bar for leadership is if you source people for your team who have different lived experiences from your own. This is a more advanced notion of inclusion, and when team members aren't all thinking with the same mind or coming from the same backgrounds, it will benefit your work tremendously. In my experience, the highest-achieving teams are made up of people with disparate perspectives who can respectfully disagree with each other and productively interrogate each other's thought processes.

It goes back to that question of "How do you like to be challenged?" How do you like to be held to a standard? Pushed to train more rigorously? Sharpen your skills more aggressively? Deepen your impact on the world? Athletes who never get challenged don't become professional athletes; similarly, leaders who never get challenged don't rise to the heights they otherwise could.

And just in case you're thinking, "But I'm a leader who never gets challenged because I always know what's best," consider the possibility that you have not created a work environment where people feel safe to speak up and give you their valuable insights. Get ready for some tough love: To manifest that feeling of safety in a work environment, you as a leader must set aside your ego-driven desire to provide all the answers for everybody else.

Pro tip: Let other people be the heroes. Let a teammate be the one to voice the amazing idea or get credit for the solve, and resist the urge to chime in and say that you were already thinking the same thing. (If you listen to group discussions, you'll notice how many times people try to retroactively share credit for something that's already been approved. But a secure person doesn't chase after credit.) Encourage people to believe in themselves, show them that their ideas are sought after and meaningfully included, and they will perform infinitely better. This brings immediate rewards to you as a leader and generates sustainable improvements in your team through a cycle of positive reinforcement.

When I became a showrunner, I was able to center the value of inclusion in my own leadership and engineer an environment where others could find it for themselves. On *Nancy Drew* and our spin-off *Tom Swift*, I was entirely intentional and effective in hiring people with a multitude of intersectional identities. For *Tom Swift*, we had an additional interest in sourcing authentic voices to help tell the story of a gay Black billionaire who is a genius inventor.

From the writers to the people in front of the camera to the people behind the scenes, we conducted an exhaustive recruitment process that gathered the most joyfully varied group of humans I've ever collaborated with. Everyone knew that they had been chosen for their unique lived experiences as well as their professional skills, so they felt that much more excited about contributing their innovations and talents to the show. As a result, even on our relatively limited budget, we put a beautiful series on the air that profoundly resonated with audiences who were eager to have their own identities and histories celebrated and explored on screen.

With that as the precious world that our warm, inclusive, two-hundred-person production team had made, it was especially heartbreaking when our show was canceled in the wake of The CW network's purchase by Nexstar. But my journey in shaping the culture of *Tom Swift* proved to me how prioritizing inclusion would elevate the creative product and develop a workplace where people wanted to stay forever and give 1000 percent every day—where people told me it was the *kindest* place they had ever been. It showed me that I could take my practices forward into the world. And the loss of *Tom Swift*, painful as it was, lit a fire in me to find an even broader canvas on which to paint my message—that canvas's latest iteration being this book.

Executive Highlights: Inclusion

This section is for those of you who enjoy recaps, and also for those of you who think you're too important to read the start of this chapter. (Or maybe you're pressed for time; I get it. You can always go back for in-depth thoughts later.)

Snack-sized takeaway: Radically including your team members will prompt heightened performance from them and better success overall. The benefit of inclusion also comes from seeking out ideas and contributions from a team with varied lived experiences and incorporating their ideas and contributions to support your goals.

Business benefit: Meaningfully including others and acknowledging the fact that people have provided their ideas and efforts at your request will connect them emotionally to their jobs. As a result, they'll work harder for you, with increased longevity and loyalty, and sometimes even with enjoyment (which in turn leads to more longevity and loyalty in team members, as a reminder to any humorless taskmasters who don't give a rat's ass about enjoyment).

Sustainable strategy: Offer clarity to those around you concerning how their efforts support the vision and endgame of the entire organization, and normalize the habit of offering this clarity. Connect the dots for everyone about how their piece of the puzzle supports the mandates and impact of the team as a whole; this incentivizes individuals to care and excel.

Seriously, try this at home: When you receive an email, reply to it with "Received" or another appropriate acknowledgment within one business day. It's astonishing how many leaders neglect to do this.

Even if you're not the boss yet: You can still model, foster, and sustain inclusive leadership. Get respectfully curious about other team members' backgrounds and perspectives. Ask colleagues for their opinions and thoughtfully consider what they have to offer on every level. Make sure to give people credit for their ideas. With productive and professional questions, ask your supervisor and teammates to provide context for why you're all doing what you're doing. By asking those questions, you'll help normalize the practice of inclusion for everyone around you.

To lead with inclusion, you'll have to expand your tolerance for the discomfort of *bringing others into your space*. "Space" meaning the headspace, physical environment, ideation process—all the places where we get protective and defensive about the specialness of our domains. It may feel odd and unfamiliar at first to invite varied viewpoints and voices into the inner sanctum of what you've been guarding professionally, or what your workplace culture has always held to be the rarefied provenance of only a few. However, I promise that when you let a wide range of people in and sincerely welcome their contributions, your work will radically deepen, with corresponding payoffs as results.

PS. Here's the surprise in all my strategies: You don't have to be in a leadership position to use these tactics like a leader. No matter where you are in the ecosystem of an organization or in a web of personal relationships, you can act with these intentions and change dynamics for the better. That change can start with your household, spread into your workplace, and ripple out into the world. (I also never said I was an underacheiver.)

But wait, there's more: To find out how the core value of all of these leadership skills—namely, kindness—can be put into action as your secret, world-changing superpower, read on....

CHAPTER 2

KINDNESS COMES FROM THE TOP

"In my fifteen years in the business,
you're the first producer who has
ever asked me what my name was."

*—A TV crewmember's response after I
extended a handshake and said hello*

My younger son recently asked if I was nice to people because I was hoping they'd like me. I admitted to him that in my twenties that was part of what motivated me; I was certainly raised to be a people pleaser, and it took me many years of trial and error to pivot away from those ingrained habits. But now that I am decades older and have much less anxiety about whether people like me or not, I have found that being kind is its own reward.

The words "kind" and "nice" are not interchangeable. Here's how I distinguish between the two. Being nice is achievable through social interactions featuring cheerful politeness, pleasant smiles, breezy compliments, hearty encouragement, minor lies to spare people's feelings, and so on. (I've also just described the experience of attending an entertainment industry cocktail party in LA.) Anyone can act nice for short periods of time, and most people want to be perceived as being nice. But it takes much more intentionality and effort to be consistently *kind* over long periods of time and during stressful situations, and when nobody is looking and there is no foreseeable good feeling that comes back to you as a result. That experience can be a lonelier one.

Lonely or not, I firmly believe that being kind is the best way to interact with others, and I've also seen *the concrete and sustainable business benefits of being kind.* Here are some examples of intentional kindness when applied with professionalism and courtesy:

- giving an employee a candid review about how they're not meeting expectations
- letting an employee go from a job that they're underperforming in and unsuited for
- respectfully and promptly telling someone that their project is not one that you can get involved in, even though you know your participation would be incredibly helpful to them

You're not being kind if you're "protecting" someone from necessary feedback; you're actually setting them up for failure by not giving them a road map to improve. You're not being kind by keeping someone in a position where they're not going to be able to thrive, excel, or get promoted; you're just putting a strain on the rest of the team while they pick up the slack for their underperforming colleague, and you're draining valuable morale in the process. You're not being kind by being unclear (or worse, silent) about whether you're going to say yes or no to a project; you're wasting people's valuable time when they could be doing far more productive things than waiting for you to articulate your position.

If these examples sound uncomfortable and challenging, that's because the title of this book is not *Lead with Kindness: You'll Always Feel Cozy!* However, take heart. Even if it's difficult in the moment, kindness will still lead to improved connection and productivity from your team. And, great news: Sometimes being kind also feels good. Plus, it can often be quite simple, with rewards that far outweigh a minimal investment of effort up front. This chapter offers strategies for kind engagement with the people around you. It starts with literally saying hello.

Here's some context for how I developed my interpersonal approach in my job as a TV producer. As in many professional cultures where ego and fear intersect, Hollywood tends to find ways to externalize hierarchy. For example, the average film set feels like a medieval court. On any given night in Vancouver, you'll find members of leadership teams (director, producer, writer, cinematographer, and so on) in tents warmed by heaters provided by the production company, while a few yards away, the hair stylists and makeup artists huddle in camp chairs they brought from home, and a few yards away from that, production assistants shiver on their feet all night.

This is less than kind, and I ask the locations department to set up additional heated tents when possible, but providing a chair and a heater is only one way to let people know you value their contributions. An even more meaningful way is to initiate a conversation with them and listen.

During production, I like to eat lunch with the crew and pick a random table to sit down at so I can get to know people over a meal, find out how they came to be in their current job, and—most importantly—learn what their aspirations are. Everyone on a crew is doing this work because they're a storyteller at heart. When I walk onto a set, I see two hundred *storytellers* who share the common goal of making our TV show awesome so that we can reach and lift up millions of audience members with our narrative, thematic, and emotional impact.

The most essential practice of my kindness-in-leadership philosophy is this: Acknowledge that people are doing the thing you asked them to do.

This can be done with eye contact and a nod or an email reply that says "Received." (If you have it in you, I recommend going beyond this by smiling when you make eye contact and saying, "Thank you," as well as "Received." But believe it or not, "Received" will do the trick.) It doesn't matter what the task is; all the tasks are important. On set, the person who maintains the portable restrooms is crucial. Without that person, the production shuts down. When I see that person servicing the trailers, I make sure to introduce myself and then continue to greet them and thank them by name every time I see them.

This is not the norm for showrunners or even writer-producers on set. I attribute other producers' standoffishness to a lack of perspective about the commitment-building benefits of my approach. Producers might perceive themselves as too busy, too self-conscious, or too important to make the effort of individually greeting each crew member. They also might want to emphasize the difference in hierarchy in an attempt to make people fear for their jobs—counting on that anxiety to make subordinates stay in line.

But in my experience, when people are treated like faceless underlings, that's the level of performance you get in return. And you can force people to tiptoe around when you generate an atmosphere of insecurity, but that culture of tiptoeing takes a massive collective toll on the energy that everyone should instead be devoting to your shared goals.

I shared my operational style with a class of new showrunners at the Writers Guild Showrunner Training Program recently, and then a few months later received a handwritten thank-you note from one of those showrunners. He had taken my advice and learned each crew member's name and said hello and thank you to them whenever he saw them. He described how Joanna the security guard lit up every morning when he greeted her by name on his way into the studio lot and confirmed that this single change in his approach to the crew had fostered both harmony and outstanding work—because *when you show kindness, it lifts morale and then people try harder for you.*

The new showrunner's account confirmed that my techniques are learnable and spreadable. I keep his thank-you note in a place of honor; his kindness helped spur me to write this book, and if that's not a measurable business result, I don't know what is.

A quick regroup on kindness strategies:

1. Look people in the eye.
2. Learn their names.
3. Acknowledge that they are doing the work you asked them to do.

It's not rocket science.
At least, this part isn't.

⊕

Not every environment is conducive to kindness, which makes kindness all the more crucial in the human interactions that result. Let's look at some causes and effects from an extremely unkind environment: prison.

Case Study: The Ride Home Program

Yes, actual prison, where people live behind bars for months, years, and decades. For the purposes of this discussion, I'm simply going to highlight some neutral facts and some evidence-based findings.

- Neutral facts: While incarcerated, people are subjected to institutional restrictions that minimize an individual's sense of self. After completing a prison sentence, many people return to their communities without the skills or support systems to sustain a stable life. This can lead to actions that land them back in prison (a technical word for this is "recidivism").
- Evidence-based findings: When people leave prison, if they are shown intentional kindness, that kindness exponentially increases their chances for successfully reintegrating into society and *not returning to prison.*

The Anti-Recidivism Coalition (ARC) is a robust nonprofit in Los Angeles that provides support and advocacy for people who have been incarcerated. Its offices are airy and bright, with exposed brick, high ceilings, and natural light. This is part of how the ARC puts kindness into action: by creating an environment that tells their clients that they are valuable and worthy human beings.

In these spacious and well-designed offices, ARC staff provide a wide variety of support services around housing, job searches, mental health, and navigating the parole system. Regular follow-ups, mentor pairings, and support groups help clients deal with day-to-day challenges and practical needs, as well as the long-term psychological impact of incarceration. ARC also operates the Ride Home Program, which puts kindness into action for people who have just been released from prison, with measurable reductions in recidivism in the population it serves.

Say you're someone who has just completed your sentence of forty-six years in prison, and you're being released from a correctional facility in Northern California at 3 a.m. You'll be given $200 and told to report to a court-mandated residential reentry center in Los Angeles. However, you no longer have friends or family members who will pick you up when you step outside of the prison walls. That's where the Ride Home Program comes in.

Through this program, a member of the ARC community will meet you at whatever time you're being released, and they'll give you a ride to your next destination—even if that destination is a ten-hour drive away. As part of your reentry, your ARC mentor will treat you to your first meal.

"The first meal is anything you've been thinking about, that you've seen on TV, or you heard people talking about," said Ride Home cofounder Carlos Cervantes. "Before picking someone up, we get on the phone and spend fifteen to twenty minutes talking about how it's all going to go, and then we ask the crucial question: Where do you want to eat? Some people pick Wingstop. Most people choose cheeseburgers; I don't know why. And after we pick people up, we sit down and have a meal together. In prison, you have two minutes to eat. So, it's important that we have time to sit down and decompress."

(When I spoke with Cervantes, I had to ask him to clarify—what did he mean by having "two minutes to eat"? Turns out he meant it literally. He explained to me that in prison, you might have 1,500 people moving through the line in a mess hall that can only fit so many people. In this scenario, you walk in with an eight-ounce plastic cup and a plastic spoon. After you get your plastic tray of food and a cup of Kool-Aid or water, you sit down and you have two minutes to eat everything. Then you have to make room for the next people coming in. You give the tray back, and you leave the mess hall with just your plastic cup and spoon. On your way out, if you get found with food in your pockets—because the correction officers will pat you down if they see any bulges that look like hidden food—you can get written up, and they can delay your next board-of-parole hearing by thirty days.)

So, there you are after being released from prison, having just been picked up by someone from the ARC's Ride Home Program, and now you're sitting down and eating a meal that lasts longer than two minutes for the first time in forty-six years. The Ride Home mentor asks questions like what you want to do for a job, what help you need with family reunification, what you want to accomplish in three months, and what you want to accomplish in three years.

"On our side, we have to sit there and be patient and soak it up," said Cervantes. "One of the biggest things is to be compassionate, to be caring. But beyond that, we have a civic responsibility as a community to see that these people have the resources that they need to come out of this system that has been cruel to them and has thrown them away up 'til now."

On the receiving side of the ride home, the impact is immediate and profound. Former ARC client Paul (not his real name) remembered when Cervantes picked him up after he was released from incarceration. Paul recalled, "I went in when I was twenty, and you come out when you're fifty-four—there were a lot of changes. Getting a social security card, applying for a job—it's all online. But you know nothing about going online. Someone can give you the benefit of his wisdom like Cervantes did. [It's] not [from] someone who can tell you about what they read in a book, or a parole officer telling you what you better do, but [coming from] someone who had experienced it themselves, and had experienced success, [it] was so helpful." He remembered how he felt during that ride with Cervantes: "I was trying to pretend I was relaxed and comfortable, but…I was scared to death."

Paul found the Ride Home experience so meaningful that he eventually became a driver for the program himself. He said that the many hours spent together on that first day are a key to the program's efficacy. In addition to the drive, there's time spent eating, shopping for clothes, and talking about how to navigate the return to a community.

Paul remembered one client whose initial bravado about returning home faded at the end of this long day. "We sat down, and I could see him start to tear up. He said, 'I don't have a job, I don't have a place to go—I've been gone twenty-seven years, and so much has changed.' And I could tell him my story and say I was there, and I felt the same way. It's really beneficial. I worked with fifty or sixty people in the two years I was with the program, and none of them returned to custody."

Paul still talks to some of the people he gave a ride home to between 2016 and 2018. One person is in culinary school, another works construction, another is in the landscaping business. Those connections came out of Paul guiding them through their first day after their release. He remembered that when he coached clients about what they needed to do for themselves, their friends, their families, and their communities, it would remind him of the standards he needed to hold himself to. Paul's kindness towards others helped him stay centered while he rebuilt and restarted his own life post-incarceration.

The ARC's work has a similar impact on many clients. In 2023, ARC members who were supported by the Ride Home Program and their other services experienced a 10 percent recidivism rate, compared to the statewide recidivism rate of 60 percent. In other words, the ARC's kindness is literally keeping people out of prison—starting from the moment when a client sits down to experience the human dignity of eating an unhurried meal for the first time in forty-six years.

Reflecting on that first meal that an ARC client enjoys after being released from prison, I noticed three transferable actions into the workplace.

1. The meal is an external way to remind this person of their intrinsic worth. That's what kindness does in the workplace too. But it's far too often neglected, and so its huge benefits go unreaped.

2. The meal offers the investment of meaningful time, at the pace of a human being. It's not about efficiency. Instead, the intentionality of the time spent is what makes it a game changer.

3. The meal is an interaction where you show respect for this person's lived experience by being open to their personal history, their anxieties, and their hopes.

their complaints about their lives. (Easier said than done, I know. But think of the time you'll free up.) Healthy boundaries = better headspace = better work results.

If that seems like a lot of self-care items, take an inventory of how many daily stressors are actively using up your energy. Five examples off the top of my head:

- commuting in traffic
- mentally spiraling about a problem that is beyond your control
- worrying about a loved one's health or your own health
- striving to meet an immovable deadline
- working within a system that is not aligned with your core values

To make this entirely reductive, you can look at your stressors as obstacles to your work productivity, and you can look at your self-care practices as highly effective counteragents to the stressors in your life. By mitigating stress with self-care, you reallocate emotional and mental energy to be more productive at work. In other words, kindness is good for business.

Self-care and kindness to yourself are strategic moves that will help you sustain internal calm, see more clearly what needs to be done, and wisely make the choices that are available to you. (Business benefits and strategies around calm are the subject of chapter 5.)

Self-care doesn't mean self-indulgence. It means shepherding the precious resources of your own time, physical energy, and mental health. You'll need those resources if you're going to succeed in your career, not to mention if you're going to nurture your personal life as well. You'll especially need those resources if you want to move beyond treading water in your current situation—that is, if you want to level up and make radically positive changes in the workplace (and world) around you.

⊕

Back to our earlier question: How can you change the culture in a place where people are not kind to each other? Let's say you've already practiced self-care, you've been kind to yourself, and you've gotten your head clear enough to make the choice to foster kindness in an unkind environment.

Here are some environments that qualify as unkind:

- A sports team where bullying behaviors have become widespread because people are imitating their dominant role models, such as coaches, star players, and parents.
- A workplace where microaggressions are commonplace. (Microaggressions are subtle instances of bias against people from marginalized groups—for example, interrupting women during a meeting while letting men finish their sentences.)
- A group chat that was created to build community among peers but instead ended up undermining trust because the most vocal and opinionated texters hijacked the thread with antagonistic comments and ego-driven agendas.

Sadly, this list could go on and on, even if we limited our examples to workplace or workplace-adjacent settings. But the human dynamics of unkind environments have several things in common: a lack of empathy, an inertia that keeps the status quo in place, a lack of negative consequences for being unkind, a lack of positive consequences for being kind, and a lack of examples of how to act with kindness.

That last one is especially important. And, crucially, those examples don't have to come from the leader of the group, though that's a far quicker route to improving the group's culture. The main thing is that it's not enough to tell people what *not* to do. It's essential to model for them what *to* do.

Here's the difference:

Telling people what not to do	vs.	Modeling kind actions
"Don't be a bully."		Offer encouragement to team members. Only speak in a respectful tone of voice. Seek consent and consensus from others without insisting on having your way. Maintain your composure.
"Don't interrupt."		Listen attentively, wait for a person to finish their thought, and then constructively echo back something that connected with you. If someone else interrupts, politely ask them to let the first person finish.
"Stop venting on the text thread."		Ask the venter if you can have a conversation with them (one-on-one, and ideally in person) about the text thread. Neutrally recap the shared goal of the text thread (increased sense of community) and, in a nonjudgmental way, ask them to limit their text messages to communications that increase community. In your own texts on the thread, only contribute in a way that increases the feeling of community.

If you just had a knee-jerk reaction of "that's so much *work* to be patient and constructive with everyone, especially people who have just pissed me off! Why do I have to be the one who's evolved? I don't have time for all these words and steps! Can't I just tell them to stop and shut up?" then your feelings are entirely human. But if you let your feelings and frustrations drive the bus, then your leadership is subpar because people will learn not to trust or respect you because of your lack of emotional self-regulation, and I'm guessing you'd rather not be subpar.

Deep breath: When you model kindness by responding in a constructive, calm, and thoughtful way—no matter what the circumstance or provocation—you will gain others' respect for your leadership. It does take more work, and you will have to bite your tongue sometimes, but the payoffs are entirely worth it.

These actions might seem basic, but they don't come naturally to everyone out there.

The standards of professionalism have been long forgotten or ignored in some environments, especially in places that operate under intense pressures of time, scrutiny, budget, and ego.

And it might take more than one conversation and many instances of modeling to reach your goal of instilling kind behavior in others.

But the change has to start somewhere, and it can most easily start with you. (It's fastest to change your own behavior and make your own choices, after all.) The key is to *take action and model kindness*, because if you leave an unkind environment alone, it will either stay the same or, very likely, get worse.

Recap on how to start changing unkind environments into kind ones:

1. Model kind actions in order to set an example for others to follow.
2. Model kind actions in order to raise empathy levels in those around you.
3. Model kind actions in order to break the inertia that was allowing unkind behavior.

But what about changing the other two elements I mentioned in unkind environments—namely, enforcing negative consequences for being unkind and providing positive consequences for being kind?

While kind examples, empathy-building, and inertia-breaking can come from anyone and everyone on the team, the enforcement of consequences is usually the purview of the leader. Hopefully, that's you. Even if it isn't, let's dream for a minute.

A clarification on what I mean by negative consequences. I don't mean public condemnation or a monetary fine, although if you look at lawsuits in Hollywood, those consequences (which sometimes play out in the national media with multimillion-dollar settlements) would seem to be the only things that move the needle in getting people to think twice before harassing their colleagues in violation of labor laws and basic decency.

I'm actually suggesting something much less incendiary. I'm suggesting that if you're a leader and you see someone on your team behaving in an unkind way, you have a measured, documented conversation where you specify what the behavior was and why it doesn't meet your minimum standard of professionalism.

For example, "You yelled at a colleague on the phone this morning. That doesn't meet my minimum standard of professionalism." Then you request a different specific behavior (in this case, no yelling), and document that request (and the team member's response to your request) as well. Also set a metric for how to measure success, such as "no more yelling, ever."

You'll also have to be clear about what happens if the yelling continues, and here I'm just going to blue-sky a scenario. For instance, if the yelling continues, the employee will be put on probation and given two weeks to show they can do their job without yelling. If they can't refrain from yelling at colleagues for two weeks, then they should start looking for another job.

I realize that most work ecosystems are more complex than what I'm describing. (Then again, imagine the difference it would make if in every workplace in this country people chose not to yell at each other anymore, ever.) Anyway, the core of the idea is that you need to tell people—as in, say it to them out loud, and document the specifics of what you said—how you want them to behave in the workplace, and let them know what will happen if they don't perform at the level of your professional and reasonable expectations.

By the way, this should apply in a 360-degree manner. If a team member sees a leader behaving in an unkind way, the culture of the work environment should allow them to say that the leader is not meeting the minimum standard of professionalism for this team. The request for a specific change in behavior, accompanying metrics for success, and stated consequences for not hitting those metrics, should also apply.

Document all of these conversations, in case the issue persists and in case further action is required. Documentation can be as simple as sending an email to yourself about the conversation; this records the specifics, the people involved, and the timeline should you need to provide information in a formal investigation of any kind.

All that said, in my experience, negative consequences—though sometimes necessary to enforce—are not nearly as effective as *positive consequences.*

Finally, something pleasant! Well, positive consequences can absolutely be pleasant, but the larger goal is creating a self-sustaining culture of humane and respectful interactions. So, this section isn't about having parties, prizes, or physical incentives to reward kind behavior (though I would not discourage any of those things). No, this section is about intangible rewards for kindness. It's about incentivizing kind behavior by tapping into what motivates unkind behavior and pivoting it.

Let me take you through my thought process.

Like many humans, I sometimes browse the internet, and I was recently struck by some really unkind interactions online. This happened to be internet chatter about a celebrity who was having a fall from grace. There was an accompanying group of at-home commentators who were piling onto the criticisms and posting conjecture that may not have been based in truth but that was doing plenty of damage regardless.

My theory is that these online antagonists, like most bullies, are driven by a desire to feel importance, agency in the world, and public recognition. With that in mind, what if we could give people in the workplace those same emotional rewards for acting with kindness?

In other words, in addition to modeling kind behavior as a leader, you should immediately take note of and reward kind behavior in your team members. These rewards should generate the same sense of importance, agency, and amplification that bullies can get through their bad behavior. But instead of getting those things through hurting others, your team members will get those rewards by being kind towards others. Here's how you can be the conduit for those validating feelings:

- Giving someone a sense of importance: Let your team member know that because of their kind behavior, you'd love to hear more about where they are in their career journey and answer any questions they might have about the work you're doing together. This offers the reward of *access* to you, the leader.
- Giving someone agency in the world: Let your team member know that you respect their kind behavior so much that you'd like to hear their suggestions about the shared work of the team. And then act on at least one of those suggestions. This offers the reward of *influence* in a larger sphere than they previously had.
- Giving someone public recognition: Let your team member know how much you appreciate their kind behavior, and commend them publicly (this doesn't have to be with a lot of fanfare—it can just be a casual name-check during a meeting or an acknowledgment within an email to the whole team). This offers the reward of *visibility* while they're praised among their colleagues.

In sum, despite what the internet might sometimes indicate about the amount of kindness people exhibit these days, I am doubling down on being kind, and I believe that it's possible to create a long-term shift towards kind behavior in others. Maybe I'm doing this in reaction to our current world. But I know kindness works. I know it brings increased happiness, calm, and success. And I want those things for you too. That's why I wrote this book.

I have always found that kindness is its own reward. But if self-interest is your on-ramp, then be kind for self-serving reasons—*being kind will make you and your team more productive, more efficient, and more accomplished.* Meanwhile, with continued practice, you might also find that the experience of being kind is worth it in and of itself. That's my hope for you, anyway.

Executive Highlights: Kindness

This section is especially for the skeptics who were too cool to read an entire chapter on kindness but who are still worried about missing out on any tactical workplace advantages enumerated therein.

Snack-sized takeaway: Acting with kindness towards others is a smart and powerful business move. If someone in your orbit is being unkind, model kind behavior and request that they follow your example. Document these requests. Clarify what the negative and positive consequences are for unkind and kind behavior, and follow through on those consequences.

Business benefit: Being kind to people—by which I mean treating them with minimum respect and decency and therefore professionalism—helps calm their nervous systems and free up precious resources of mental and emotional energy. Calm, energetic people work more effectively. Effective workers reach (your) goals more efficiently.

Sustainable strategy: Communicate gratitude for the combined efforts of your team on a consistent basis. Example: When you email the group, include the phrase "Thanks, all." When other team members act with kindness, reinforce positive consequences for them—such as a FaceTime with you, acting on their suggestions, and publicly acknowledging their kind actions.

Seriously, try this at home: Learn the names of people you wouldn't normally greet—a parking attendant, your mail carrier, a grocery store checkout clerk (they wear nametags, which gives you a low barrier to entry). And then address them directly and thank them by name for their help, like: "Thanks, Bobbie!" I guarantee that the word "thanks," plus their name, plus eye contact, will noticeably improve their day and yours.

Even if you're not the boss yet: With discernment, spend less time *acting nice*. Niceness, especially manufactured niceness that's secretly motivated by not wanting to be truthful towards another person, takes up energy (often because of the draining effects of trying to prevent awkwardness for yourself and everyone around you). Reallocate that energy and use it to *be kind* instead. Kindness—including the tough-love variety in service of a shared goal—keeps your actions targeted at having a lasting, positive impact in the world.

To lead with kindness, you'll have to expand your tolerance for the discomfort of *humility*. Kindness boils down to showing others that they have intrinsic worth as human beings, which means their intrinsic worth is no less than yours. That's a great leveler, and the best foundation for respectful connection, but it's a connection that comes from your common humanity, not from a hierarchical bond. The good news is this: What you release in ego, you get back tenfold in shared respect.

But wait, there's more: For kindness and inclusion to work at full power in a group dynamic, you first need to create receptivity to these practices—which can only happen when you foster and (re)build an atmosphere of trust. To find out how to do that, read on....

CHAPTER 3

TRUST = PERFORMANCE

"It's so interesting that you people
have to work in teams, and yet
you don't seem to understand
the concept that well."

This is what a good friend (not from the entertainment industry) said upon hearing my accounts of many past work experiences where the top person or couple of people on the TV writing staff would disappear behind closed doors and insist on doing all the work by themselves. It would leave the rest of us frustrated, demoralized, and sidelined while we wondered what the hell was going on. If this sounds like an experience you've been on the receiving end of, my sympathies. If this sounds like an experience you've given to others because you thought it was the best solution for everyone, then I have a more productive pathway to suggest: *Trust people.*

I'm talking about genuinely trusting people. Like, truly relying upon them to do what you need them to do without your constant supervision and control. This means you'll have to get a clear commitment from your team member (more on this in chapter 8 on accountability), and then you'll need to walk away and let them take ownership of what you've delegated to them.

If that prospect elicits instinctive resistance or possibly mild terror, then this chapter is definitely for you. No judgment, of course. I totally understand what it is like to have had life and work experiences that have left you disinclined to trust those around you. I completely believe that you are a highly competent and accomplished person who has thus far succeeded by relying only on yourself. I also acknowledge that you may find yourself in an environment where trust among coworkers has been badly damaged or broken, leaving real and lasting wounds. In any and all of those scenarios, you might think it's actually a business advantage to be distrustful of those around you.

Incorrect! Trust is good for business, especially when it's trust that you foster among your team members so they can work together cohesively, committedly, and unreservedly in pursuit of your shared goals.

As another motivation for your workplace, if there's been a systemic breakdown in trust—for instance, if the team's time and boundaries are routinely disrespected, if people grab credit for their colleagues' work, if the group dynamic can be accurately described as "snake pit"—then you need to intervene. Until you correct the underlying culture, results will not improve. Having worked in more than one snake pit myself, I can tell you that the quality and quantity of work produced was only a fraction of what the team would have accomplished if the distrust in the environment had not forced us into foxholes of bitterness and self-protection.

After trust has been broken, how can you restore trust, and how can you get good at trusting people going forward? And how can you help those around you trust each other as well?

The process will require effort. But I promise the benefits are crucial and paradigm shifting. And there are practical and doable steps you can take in order to build and restore trust.

$\oplus$

Before I get into those skills and tactics, though, I'm going to sidebar for a moment about an aspect of trust that can be deeply uncomfortable to us leader types. That aspect is *vulnerability*. But don't let your discomfort keep you from engaging with this, because of this truth:

> **Vulnerability is not weakness. Vulnerability is a bridge to connection. Only with real connection can you build real trust.**

With those words staring back at you, you might be thinking, "That's okay. I'll settle for wary trust or half-trust, because I never want to show or experience vulnerability—then I could get taken advantage of, or be thought less of, or otherwise indicate to my coworkers that I am not an actual god. I'll just tough it out and continue to resist being vulnerable, thanks."

Folks! Release those doubting thoughts. We are here for a better way forward—a better way that will net you greater success and career advancement, Overworked Businessperson. But the better way forward requires you to step out of your comfort zone.

Stepping out of your comfort zone might include acknowledging the fact that if there is a lack of trust in your current working relationships, part of that lack of trust might be coming from your end. As in, you're not willing to be vulnerable in order to invite people's trust.

I don't know who you work with, and I don't know what your particular emotional past is. And even with those variables aside, I understand that trusting people, and asking them to trust you, does carry a degree of risk. Anything unknown can be a little bit scary. It can be nerve-racking to deliberately put yourself into situations where you can't control how others will behave or respond around your vulnerability (by which I mean your openness and your willingness to connect).

But when you consistently hold yourself to a standard of professional behavior that is above reproach, then you have nothing to hide and nothing to prove. When you come from that place of your own integrity, your openness will disarm people—both on an interpersonal level and in the sense of giving them no ammunition to use against you. Maybe they'll call you earnest. There are much worse things to be called.

If the above exhortations aren't sufficient to change your lens on this yet, then humor me and do yourself a favor: *Pretend* that you are a person who is not threatened by being vulnerable. And then act accordingly. It'll be worth it.

Okay. Now that you are mindfully embracing your vulnerability and openness to fostering genuine bonds of trust with others (or at least you're acting as if you are a person who could apply this strategy), let's get back to the steps that will help you build that trust.

The following three steps are not the only steps you can take, but they stand out to me from my many years of leadership and parenting (so these methods are battle-tested). The key to all of this is integrity—by which I mean being honest in what you say while also showing respect for others in what you do. But along with being an honorable person, you have to *put your integrity into action with consistency, connection, and understanding.* Let's go step-by-step.

Step 1: Trust is built through applying integrity with consistency.

To build trust, it's crucial to prove to your team that you can be consistent (and consistent in ways that benefit them, of course). One effective tactic: Say you're going to do something and then actually do it. Over and over. People need to see that your word has meaning. When you show your team that your statements can be taken at face value, that builds trust, and it can also help rebuild trust that has been broken.

What kinds of statements can have the most immediate impact, you wonder? So glad you asked. Here's a very effective way to earn trust: Tell your team that you will start meetings on time and end meetings on time, and then actually follow through on that.

When I say *start meetings on time*, I'm not just talking about clicking on the Zoom link or being seated in the conference room when the big hand hits the hour on the clock (though this is part of it). I'm talking about getting into the substance of your meeting immediately, or as close to immediately as humanly possible, after a one- or two-minute welcome to set a cordial tone and thank everyone for their presence. This means skipping the handful(s) of minutes that can so easily be frittered away with chitchat, refilling coffee, complaining about something off topic, and so on.

Think of all the seven-minute-long stretches of *nothing* that have begun so many of the meetings you've attended. I would bet real money that I've sat through a hundred meetings that began like that. Seven times a hundred is seven hundred minutes that I could have spent doing anything else. And if you, the leader, are wasting hundreds of minutes multiplied by the number of people in those meetings, then that adds up to days and weeks of your team's valuable productivity that you let slip away. When people know that their time is being wasted, that drains trust from the environment. Start meetings on time!

The other thing that happens when you don't start the meeting on time is that you end up training people to know that they can slink in six minutes late and miss absolutely nothing. This detracts from the focus in the room and disrespects the time and effort of those who showed up punctually. That drains trust from the environment as well. In contrast, when you are focused and in the flow of the meeting at two minutes past the hour, people learn that they need to be ready and on their game at the stated meeting time. Just as importantly, they learn that when you say the meeting starts at 10 a.m., you mean it, and your actions follow through on your words.

I also urge you to give your team a fixed and *dependable end time for every meeting* so that they can plan the rest of their lives from that point forward. For instance, if you have a daily meeting that is scheduled to end at 12:30 p.m., and you are scrupulous and rigorous about actually ending the meeting when you promised it would end, then people can plan their next meeting, their next task, their travel time to lunch or errands outside the office—all activities that will give them agency as human beings, reduce their stress, and train them to be better leaders themselves.

Note that I used the word "promise" in regards to ending a meeting on time. Every time your meetings trail past the scheduled end time, you are breaking a promise to your staff, and on a subconscious level you are telling your team, over and over and over and over, that your word means nothing. This is a fixable issue and one with incredible impact on the dynamic in your workplace.

The fixed end-time for every meeting has an additional benefit. If you're not able to get through everything you need to do by that end point, with an eye on the clock about fifteen minutes prior to the scheduled end, tell folks that it doesn't look like you'll be able to get done by the scheduled end time. So, you're going to need to schedule an additional meeting to cover the unfinished items. You will be surprised how efficiently people move when they realize that whatever they don't finish by the scheduled time, they'll have to reconvene to discuss again. With open-ended meetings that have no declared end-time, there's much less incentive to keep things moving.

As you continue to be consistent and exhibit integrity in this one practice—start on time/end on time—people will learn that they can take you at your word. In short, you will teach people to trust you.

The above is just one way to demonstrate consistency to your team. Globally:

Clearly state what you're going to do to benefit your team and then actually do it, over and over again. Consistency builds trust.

Follow through on your promises, over and over. Once people know they can trust you with everyday matters, they can trust you with bigger swings and more ambitious leaps of faith—which will serve all of you as an increasingly cohesive and effective team.

In addition to proving you are a dependable person who consistently delivers on your word, you'll need to encourage and sustain genuine openness among the members of your team. Here's the next step in trust-building:

Step 2: Trust is built through applying integrity with connection.

I'll start with a small example of connection. It's as simple as being respectful to everyone you encounter, no matter where they are on the org chart and even if there is no obvious Machiavellian benefit to you in return for treating them with common decency.

TV producer and former entertainment agent Lis Rowinski has built her career around relationships and trust. She remembers her early training in this crucial area: "One of the best pieces of advice I ever got upon my promotion to agent was from an executive who told me, 'There is going to be a temptation, because you just got promoted, to only reach up in your relationships. Resist the temptation to only reach up. You want to be reaching across. Reaching down. Be good to everyone, and be curious about them in a respectful way.'"

I strongly recommend this kind of holistic courtesy. If people witness you being authentically gracious with everyone around you no matter why your paths are intersecting, then they'll know they can expect the same graciousness when you interact with them, and that will build the trust between you. (In contrast, think back to a time when you were waiting for your turn at a fast-food drive-through or at the airport check-in line, and you saw someone ahead of you being a jerk to the person trying to help them. I bet you would trust that jerk less than you would trust a person who you saw being gracious in the same setting.)

If nobody witnesses you being authentically gracious with those around you, but that's how you connect with people anyway just because it's the right thing to do and it feeds your soul, I firmly believe that people will be able to sense that about you as a person, and that will build their trust in you as well. Try this out. Gracious connection feels good, especially with repetition. And:

> **Gracious connection
> builds trust.**

But what about when you're dealing with a preexisting trust dynamic that's been severely damaged by previous events and patterns? When connection itself feels nearly impossible, how can trust be repaired?

To address this, let's look at a nationwide organization's success in restoring connection and trust in seemingly unhealable relationships: those between trauma survivors and their abusers.

Case Study: Rebuilding Connection and Trust in Trauma Survivors

In 1991, Cathy Salser founded A Window Between Worlds (AWBW), a nonprofit organization that uses art as an empowering resource for people and communities impacted by violence and trauma. They currently have about 1,300 facilitators across the US, working with survivors of domestic violence, child abuse and neglect, and sexual assault. With nearly five hundred partner organizations, AWBW facilitators support mental health needs and also guide survivors in rebuilding trust with those around them, including their abusers. AWBW-trained facilitators also lead workshops to transform workplace dynamics after trust has been broken.

"Rebuilding trust is a journey," Salser told me. "It's not just one conversation. As an artist, I invite folks to anchor a journey in art and on paper. They express what's difficult about where they are now and where they hope to get moving forward…We're trying to connect and hold intentions over time. That's what's difficult in domestic violence and toxic workplaces where you have history and you don't trust."

Salser and her colleagues have found that art can be a crucial resource while people are healing in the aftermath of trauma. When people make art during their transformative journeys, that art provides a touchstone for the positive changes in their nervous systems and psychological experiences.

This goes for abusers as well as the abused. "Within domestic violence, you now work with batterers as well as victims, because you also need to work with the person who has caused harm," Salser said. "During these court-mandated sessions, sometimes the abuser is like, 'What the f--k am I doing here?' But you invite that person to use art as the window between what was difficult and where you hope to go."

Facilitators encourage participants to find answers to questions like, "What do I want?" and "What am I trying to do?" Then participants make or choose a physical touchstone about those intentions and carry the touchstone in their pocket. So, when they notice that old behaviors are getting in the way of their goals, they can literally hold on to their touchstone and get recentered.

In one example, a client (a former batterer who was in anger management training) carried his daughter's baby sock as the *why* for the path he was on. Meaning: *This is why I'm trying to change how I handle this feeling that comes up in me—I'm trying to regain custody so that I can be part of my daughter's life.*

Salser also talked about a father and teenaged daughter who had been estranged by trauma. They went to therapy together, but after multiple sessions they still didn't feel like they were being heard by each other. So, the therapist asked them to each paint a small stone that represented the past, as well as a small stone that represented their wishes for the future.

In the next session, the father and daughter were anchored by these stones when they talked to each other, because the stones represented reference points for and reminders of their fears and hopes. And then, the therapist asked them to take each other's stones home and take care of them. The dad even made a little bed for his daughter's stones and said good night to them every night, while the daughter kept the dad's stones in her clothes all week, as a way to hold his intentions close to her. When the dad and daughter arrived at their next therapy session and returned their stones to each other, they were able to connect in an entirely different way. "So, we find that the art is actually really efficient and a time-saver," Salser concluded.

Great news: You don't have to be a therapist or have any artistic skill at all in order to use these methods. The idea is to anchor yourself in a piece of art that brings you back to what your behavior is sourced from (point A) and reminds you of where you want to go (point B). If actual artwork sounds daunting, you could make something as simple as a doodle on a Post-it. The point is that the art (or Post-it) helps you plant a seed of change and have ownership of that seed, over time. You'll have evolutions during your journey of getting from point A to point B, but you can continually come back to these anchoring touchstones.

In a workplace setting, the practice of creating tangible artifacts to represent your intentions—whether on Post-its or on pocket stones—can help you create authentic connection with those around you, because you are clearly declaring where you hope to go together. Your openness and your vulnerability will build connection, which in turn builds trust.

Sidebar: If you just had a knee-jerk reaction of "WAIT WAIT WAIT you lost me. I don't have time to make pocket stones! I am a busy and important person, and I thought this was a book about succeeding in business!" then you have fallen into the human trap that so many other humans have fallen into before you. Namely, the trap of thinking that providing clarity is a waste of time. But it's the opposite of a waste of time, because:

Clarity builds trust.

If you're not willing to be clear with your team about where you want to go with them, then you are forcing them to flounder around and try to read your mind. This wastes far more time than taking five minutes to articulate intentions as a group and walk away with a physical reminder of those continuing intentions.

Stay with me on this. Physical touchstones have a different effect on us than verbal or written reminders; and if you've taken a little bit of time to actually create a physical touchstone with an accessible medium like colorful markers or modeling clay, it levels up the effect because you have ownership of a thing you created.

"There is no way I am doing *arts and crafts* in my workplace!" you might persist. "I am a serious grown-up who deals in facts!" Okay. While actual art projects can be uniquely cathartic and revealing, and I wholeheartedly endorse them, I will allow for teams who might not be able to make a quick jump from zero arts and crafts to workflow-intention arts and crafts. Here's what I propose for those folks: Make a small talisman that represents your intention, because that's the purpose the art serves. This external talisman could be as under the radar as an elastic band around your wrist. No one has to know what your talisman means to you. The point is to own a physical commitment to your own transformation. You get to carry this talisman of commitment over time and come back to it over and over—because it's not like we can flip a switch and be done with changing dynamics in the workplace or elsewhere. Transformation, like trust, is a journey.

All of that said, it's not just our own intentions that determine the health of our workplace. We sometimes find ourselves caught up in personal dynamics that seem immovable. For instance, maybe two coworkers have diametrically opposed approaches to the same situation, and neither is willing to budge because those approaches come from strong beliefs in what has worked for them in the past. Or, a leader's choices leave part of the team very unhappy, and people splinter into factions and subtly (or not so subtly) withhold help from people who aren't in their like-minded clique. Or, everyone on the team is intimidated by their controlling boss, and they've resigned themselves to slogging along at the mercy of the boss's moods and whims.

In these situations, if no one addresses the dysfunctions, the group's conflict avoidance leads to disempowerment, inefficiency, and exhaustion. Trust evaporates, leaving in its wake a divide that feels impossible to bridge. This is where our third element of trust-building comes in:

Step 3: Trust is built through applying integrity with understanding.

If you're going to foster and sustain a culture of genuine trust, it's crucial to understand that the members of your team are able and eager to contribute meaningfully *because* of who they are as opposed to in spite of who they are. If, for some reason, you don't believe that's true, and actually even if you do, I strongly suggest you sit with each member of your team and get to know them better. This also applies to asking for time to have a one-on-one conversation with a struggling leader to hear where they're coming from and ask about what's important to them. Even fifteen minutes per person will pay off exponential dividends.

I learned this strategy from director Clara Aranovich, who said that when she comes on board to direct an episode of TV, she schedules one-on-one conversations with every member of the cast—from the star of the show to the "day player" who is on set for just a few hours to deliver a couple of lines.

Before I directed my first episode of television on *Nancy Drew,* I did exactly as Aranovich suggested and Zoomed with each actor who would appear in the episode to talk about their character and hear their feedback about the script. I had been working with our core cast of series regulars for four seasons in my role as showrunner and executive producer, so we already knew each other well, but it was still extremely helpful to me to hear their insights about their characters in the new context of preparing to join them on set as their director.

When I talked to the episode's guest stars (actors playing larger roles whose names appear in the on-screen credits at the beginning of the show) and costars (actors playing smaller roles), the conversations were even more illuminating:

- If I hadn't had a fifteen-minute Zoom with the woman who played the ongoing love interest for Nancy Drew's dad, then I never would have heard Erica Cerra's thoughtful reflections on her formative experiences as a child actor and her journey back to acting as an adult.
- If I hadn't sat down for fifteen minutes with the woman who appeared in a lone scene to tell Nancy Drew that her clue trail has led to a hospital worker who's out of town on vacation, then I never would have learned that Bethel Lee is the daughter of a minister who named her after the place where Jacob dreamed of a ladder in the Bible story (naturally, Bethel and I bonded over how dismayed our traditional Asian parents were when we went into the arts).
- And if I hadn't set aside another fifteen minutes to talk with the man who was in a handful of our episodes as the prickly town judge, then I never would have heard Richard Keats's delightfully self-deprecating story about his first acting job on a daytime soap opera thirty-five

years prior. He had played a journalist interviewing one of the stars of that soap, and although it was a one-off scene, Keats gave such a committed performance that when the cameras stopped rolling, the star of the show told him wryly, "Nice job, slick," as he walked away.

With a much greater understanding of these individuals as people, by the time we arrived on set, I fully trusted them to deliver outstanding performances, and each of them did. They also trusted me to respect them for their life experiences and body of work, because I had taken the time to learn about both in a way that welcomed and encouraged them.

So, when I gave them direction (meaning, when I suggested the physical blocking of where they would be moving around in a scene, when I asked them to do the scene again but with different emotional subtext, or when I asked them to adjust the energy of a line reading because of how it fit into the scene as a whole) they trusted that my vision was built around a sincere interest in bringing out the best in their work. And because we had already gotten to know each other, we were able to skip straight to the part where we genuinely enjoyed collaborating unselfconsciously, easily, and very productively.

You can build trust with every member of your team through this practice. Schedule fifteen minutes of one-on-one time (in person is great, but video calls are totally fine) and then ask the other person about what has brought them to this moment in their lives, what their thoughts are about the work you're doing together, and what their hopes are going forward. Their experiences, insights, and goals will almost certainly impress you and surprise you in the best way. Reflect back your takeaways from what they've shared, so that they know you understand them as they want to be understood. With just fifteen minutes of time for a simple conversation, both of you will have a new foundation for trusting each other.

Invest time and attention towards finding genuine understanding with your team members. That understanding will lead to trust.

So, quick regroup on trust-building strategies:

1. Apply integrity with consistency.
2. Apply integrity with connection.
3. Apply integrity with understanding.

I deliberately phrased all three of the above steps in terms of *applying* integrity because this process requires active engagement and may entail taking actions that you are not already taking. So yes, I might be adding to your list of what you need to do during the day. But I never said the title of this book was *Lead with Kindness: Kick Back and It'll Happen By Itself!*

However, when you do make a habit of these trust-building practices and invest your attention and thoughtfulness towards the psychological security of your workplace, over time you will get exponentially more bandwidth returned to you in contributions from your team. That's because you'll be trusting your team members to handle tasks that you delegate to them, and you'll be trusting each other to keep your word and honor your commitments.

Also, when you prove yourself trustworthy as a leader and foster an environment where others can be trustworthy as well, you safeguard against "integrity leaks" (in other words, dysfunctional behaviors that would weaken trust). Intact integrity will buoy the energy of the team dynamic while you trust them to take things off *your* plate.

Trust is earned by consistently proving you are a person who delivers on agreements. It's also earned by making people feel seen, celebrating their individual identity, and creating a safe dynamic that encourages them to thrive. And it's increased by genuine delegation where you show people that you respect their judgment and welcome their contributions. This means that you open yourself to receiving input from your team so that you then can elevate the results together. In all of this, it's crucial to hold yourself to the highest possible standards of personal and professional behavior—because if you don't model that for your team, why should they behave any better than you?

When you conduct yourself with integrity, treat everyone with respect, and embrace vulnerability as a bridge to connection, your team will feel safe to voice their most daring ideas and communicate openly and professionally. This generates a more empowered collaboration, which will vastly improve the quality of the work process and its outcomes. In other words, trusting people—and being worthy of their trust in return—makes them want to help you attain all your goals.

⊕

Executive Highlights: Trust = Performance

If you skipped to the end of this chapter without reading it, hopefully it's just because you're the sort of person who skips to *The New Yorker* cartoons without reading the articles around them, and not because you're above earning your team's trust. Either way, here's a pocket guide.

Snack-sized takeaway: If people don't trust you, they won't do their best for you. Fortunately, it is entirely possible to generate and maintain trust through intentional communication, neutral listening, and consistent follow-through.

Business benefit: When the members of your team trust you and each other, they will take the leap even in the midst of uncertain circumstances and work towards your shared goals with more energy, innovation, and heart.

Sustainable strategy: When you say you're going to do something, actually do it. And do it on a stated timeline that you actually stick to. Repeat this consistently in order to build trust.

Seriously, try this at home: To gain a greater understanding of someone else's viewpoint, ask respectful questions about what matters to the *other* person, not about what matters to you. When the other person feels heard, they will trust you more.

Even if you're not the boss yet: In breakdowns of trust, use the touchstones exercise from A Window Between Worlds. Make a small, tangible reminder of the true north where you hope to reestablish trust in the future (just like the dad who'd lost custody of his infant daughter and kept one of her baby socks as a touchstone reminder to earn custody back). The more easily you can focus on your true north, the better you'll do at redirecting yourself towards it.

To lead with trust, you'll have to expand your tolerance for the discomfort of *the vulnerability of relying on other people.* This is a tough one. In fact, the reluctance/refusal to rely on other people is the source of most of the workflow bottlenecks, ego conflicts, budget overages, and other problems I've witnessed and dealt with in my twenty-three-year journey up the ranks of TV writing and production. Take a deep breath and set aside your fear, your pride, your self-consciousness about asking for help—whatever it is that's holding you back from empowering your team to do their jobs and take on more responsibility. Embrace the short-term bandwidth requirements of other people's learning curves while you truly delegate and encourage people to rise to the occasion. The long-term gain of being supported by a legitimately capable and motivated team will make your life infinitely better.

But wait, there's more: Trust is a building block for an environment where people can truly connect and be open with each other. This in turn leads to a deeper and more evolved connection to the shared goals of the group. Prepare yourself, Overworked Businessperson. That evolved connection is its own kind of (safe for work) love. Read on....

CHAPTER 4

LOVE IS A BUSINESS NECESSITY

"If you want to teach someone to become a great shipbuilder, don't teach them how to hammer a nail. Teach them to love the sea."

—*Antoine de Saint-Exupéry (paraphrased)*

In some ways this entire book started with an email that I sent to the first writer we offered a job to on *Nancy Drew*. We couldn't afford to match the salary from his previous show; the maximum we could give him was a significant pay cut from what he'd gotten elsewhere. So I humbly and transparently owned up to our budgetary limitations in the opening sentences of my email to him. I added that what I *could* offer him was an environment that was intentionally designed around humane respect and work-life integration.

My email to this writer detailed how the first three days of our writers' room would be spent with a mindfulness meditation teacher, an executive coach for team building and workplace agreements, and a service organization called Young Storytellers, where we would volunteer for a writing workshop with marginalized students in our office's neighborhood.

The rest of the email shared touchstones for my leadership practices—anecdotes ranging from how Kenneth Branagh directs (he creates an atmosphere of possibility) to how the New England Patriots were brought onto the field in the 2002 Super Bowl—not position by position with the quarterback getting the most glory, but instead as a single unified team, which at that time was revolutionary (and they won that game by a field goal, by the way). It culminated in the Saint-Exupéry quote about how one creates great shipbuilders by teaching them to love the sea. I closed the email by telling this writer that I truly hoped he would give us the chance to increase his love of the sea, because I knew if he joined our team he would only increase our love of the sea as well.

In essence, I tempted him with kindness. Specifically, I appealed to him with the promise that this was more than just a job—it was a place where he could tap into his highest personal integrity while becoming a meaningful part of a deeply worthwhile enterprise.

This writer accepted our job offer and was an integral part of the series for the four years that followed. And the moment he said yes to our lower-paying but kindness-driven show, I knew I was onto something. I realized that people were hungry for workplaces that were deliberately and thoughtfully fostering humane conditions.

But teaching people to love the sea is about more than the creation of workplace culture. Sometimes it comes easily, taught simply by the example you set when you're devoted to a passion project or when you're lucky enough to get paid to do something that fills your soul and that you would have done for free anyway. And sometimes the love of the sea—the love of a larger enterprise, the love of a shared goal, the love of a distant outcome—is taught in a much tougher environment, when you act with resilience, integrity, and dogged determination while facing incredibly challenging circumstances.

For example, what if you were a school board member in a district where a 23,448-acre wildfire burned down three of the schools under your supervision?

Case Study: The Palisades Fire and the Los Angeles Unified School District

Before I get into this case study about the powerful impact of love in the face of crisis, I will respectfully add that the Palisades fire was not the only wildfire that devastated Los Angeles County in January of 2025; the Eaton fire simultaneously burned over fourteen thousand acres in the community of Altadena and its surroundings. I've chosen to profile the Palisades fire because my younger son was a junior at Palisades Charter High School during the fire and its aftermath, so I had direct contact with Los Angeles Unified School District (LAUSD) school board member Nick Melvoin as the school began the rebuilding process. Equally determined and admirable efforts took place in Altadena following their wildfires.

Melvoin's school district contains the entirety of the Palisades. Fortunately, Palisades High was still on winter break when the fire started on January 7. Had the high school been in session that Tuesday morning, trying to evacuate three thousand kids plus all of the staff members would have been a nightmare—the school is about a hundred yards away from the part of Sunset Boulevard that you might have seen in news reports, where local residents had to abandon their cars in the evacuation gridlock and escape to safety on foot. One elementary school (Topanga) had been preemptively relocated to another campus due to the high-wind advisories, but there were still two elementary schools in session that day.

When the fire broke out, LAUSD immediately evacuated students and staff from Palisades Elementary and Marquez Elementary schools. Melvoin stayed up all night to communicate with school administrators, police, and the superintendent. The next morning, following a press conference, Melvoin drove into the Palisades with a police escort. They saw that Palisades High was about 60 percent intact, but Palisades Elementary was heavily damaged and Marquez Elementary had been completely destroyed.

After driving through areas where the general public was not yet allowed to return, Melvoin had to inform many close friends that their houses had burned to the ground. He went back to check on the school campuses on Wednesday night. He saw that there were still some embers alight in Palisades High, so he took a fire extinguisher off the wall and sprayed the glowing sparks until they went out.

He immediately started to think about contingency plans for the displaced elementary schools. Luckily, other local grade-school campuses had enough space to accommodate arriving students from Palisades and Marquez. "By Thursday, I was walking those campuses and measuring the drapes if you will," Melvoin told me. "The following Wednesday, the elementary schools were relocated and running again in person. It was remarkable to see parents and families with tears of joy that their kids were back with their peers." (The students of Palisades High, meanwhile, started their spring semester on Zoom shortly after that.)

But then, "A few weeks later, the trauma hit overwhelmingly." Once they got the kids moved to safe campuses, the LAUSD team started thinking about mental health counseling, both in person and via virtual platforms. They added a psychiatric social worker at each affected school on a full-time basis. "We also planned some joy for the kids—Disney brought characters to the colocated Marquez and Palisades student groups. Moana, the Avengers, the princesses, and Star Wars characters all came out and did a really fun day for the kids. We reminded ourselves that these are still elementary school kids."

Melvoin praised the hosting schools for their remarkable generosity and compassion, though there were significant emotional challenges along the way, especially for displaced families—and there were so many of those. In one elementary school that he toured with Governor Gavin Newsom, thirteen of seventeen kids in one class had their homes destroyed in the fires. But, Melvoin added, "We were operating with so much grace (including with staff members who had lost their own houses) that everyone was able to receive the displaced emotions from people who had lost their homes."

LAUSD hosted frequent town halls and Zooms in the months following the fires—some weeks, there were town halls for different communities every night so that people could be heard and administrators could relay updates about resources and rebuilding plans. Throughout all of this, the community's shared love for the students kept everyone focused and moving forward towards the goal of getting all three schools up and running again as soon and as safely as possible.

In the population of Palisades Charter High School, over five hundred students lost their homes in the fires; the same was true for many faculty and staff members. The school was Zoom-only until spring break, and then in the third week of April everyone (including my younger son) resumed in-person classes at the previously vacant Sears building in downtown Santa Monica. Melvoin was there for the first day at "Pali South" and remembered seeing tears of joy from the reunited kids, including seniors who were freshmen during COVID-19. Rebuilding is underway at the original Palisades Charter High School campus, and in January 2026 the students returned to their home campus, but through the end of 2025, the Sears building has served as the school's temporary home.

During the aftermath of the fires, in his personal journey from using a fire extinguisher to put out embers on a destroyed campus to welcoming thousands of high schoolers to a converted department store building, Melvoin saw the efficacy of love in action. "I've been struck by how people have come together in this crisis with so much urgency. It gives me hope for how can we do that with other things. We turned the Sears building around in three weeks," he said, referring to the expedited permits and intensive modifications needed to transform a cavernous, empty space into a working high school. To achieve this, the design and construction teams basically did three weeks of work per day.

Having seen what was possible when people were motivated for a shared goal they deeply cared about, Melvoin wondered, "How do we act and think differently about other problems in the region?"

In thinking differently and responding with love in the aftermath of natural disaster, Melvoin also highlighted the importance of working across lines of political difference. The US

Army Corps of Engineers had been instrumental in rebuilding the Palisades and so had local officials and community leaders who had not always found common ground before this crisis. By putting the kids first, Melvoin attested, people were able to work together from multiple jurisdictions. County supervisor Lindsey Horvath's office facilitated bus clearances to save kids two hours in their daily commute during the road closures that followed the wildfires, and other schools opened their campuses on weekends to provide green space for kids whose local parks had been destroyed. Schools from across the country donated textbooks and sponsored fundraising drives to support the affected communities of students. And I would argue that all of it was motivated, and made incredibly effective, by love.

As an Angeleno, I'm grateful to the many, many people around the country and the world who sent love and assistance to Los Angeles County in a multitude of ways during the 2025 wildfires and their aftermath. But you might be wondering if this kind of love is available in the everyday workplace settings that this book aims to improve. It's all very well to act with noble altruism for the common good, you might say, when there is a literal crisis at hand and folks from far and wide band together. People really do show their most generous and compassionate selves for a finite period of time. What about when your goals are not as lofty as providing a sense of normalcy for traumatized kids or as far-reaching as rebuilding a historic high school that serves three thousand students? What about when it's just everyday work that you're dealing with, when you are managing the never-ending mundane responsibilities of budget constraints and market pressures and colleagues who annoy each other?

Radical assertion: I believe it is possible to access and act as your most generous and compassionate self even when there's not an actual crisis demanding that of you. In other words, imagine what the world (and the workplace) would be like if we were as awesome to each other on an everyday basis as we are when wildfires are raging unchecked.

That said, happily, most workdays do not involve natural disasters and statewide emergencies. Let's head way back down to the everyday level, to the little interactions that build and define a workplace culture. Because it's not just that generating love is the best way forward, and it's not that love is some ethereal goal for people who have too much time on their hands. On the contrary, *generating love is a business necessity if you want to motivate your team to contribute at 100 percent of their capacity.* Because when you move to the opposite of generating love—when you disregard people, threaten them, and keep them constantly on edge—that leads to a cycle of toxicity and therefore decreased results in the workplace.

One remedy to toxicity is very simple. So simple, in fact, that it's a little sad to me that it feels necessary to put this in a business management book:

**Please say hello to each of
your team members when
they arrive for work.**

To illustrate the importance of that practice, here's a cautionary tale, provided and corroborated from multiple sources who asked to remain anonymous because of understandable fears of retaliation. Right now, inside a luxury hotel restaurant in a major city, the service is not what it used to be, because the new manager never says hello to the waitstaff as they arrive for work. She doesn't greet them or even make the tiny (though very significant) gesture of eye contact when they show up for their shift. This sets the tone because the next thing she says to the staff is always a criticism; that's another aspect of how this particular manager rolls, and it's also part of the detrimental impact on morale. Said one staff member, "It makes you want to hide from her. Also, she never acknowledges anything you do right, and you start to ascribe malice to her interactions with you. If she said hello, it wouldn't be so bad."

The lack of saying hello, admittedly, is only one part of this manager's problem. The mood of the entire team, after only a short time under the antagonistic rule of this manager, is that no one is willing to go beyond what is explicitly needed, because they know they won't be noticed for it, and they definitely won't be thanked for it.

Even worse, their experience has been that the new manager will criticize them no matter what they do—or cite consequences for mistakes that haven't happened yet or mention potential punishments for issues that have already been corrected. (An example of this manager's comments to a waitress: "I'm glad you've already replaced the shoes you had before, because I don't want to have to send you home for wearing shoes that are too casual.") If you're going to get threatened with a consequence for something you've *already corrected*, what's the point of trying to do anything more than the bare minimum?

In keeping with her emotionally destabilizing tactics, this particular manager continually intimidates team members via frontal attack. If she sees something she doesn't like, she'll go up to the waitstaff and snap, "Why would you do that?" or "Why didn't you do X?" As a result, everyone on the team is likely to throw each other under the bus because they're afraid of the manager. They won't own up to mistakes; instead, they'll hide from their mistakes and blame others for whatever happened.

"She's mean," said a staff member from the restaurant. "She's mean in how she talks about people and how she talks to people. She's made me hate my job. I used to love my job, and now I hate my job."

Another staff member left after being treated like this. "It was not worth it for me to stick around," this person told me. "I did not feel valued anymore."

Deep breath! If you're like me, the above anecdotes were rather triggering; I don't know about you, but I have worked for people who took active pleasure in harassing others and exerting dominance in ways both sweeping and insidious. So, another deep breath, and let's talk about how to fix situations like the one I just described. Good news: There is a swift approach that is as simple as it is effective:

When you acknowledge everyone you encounter as an individual human being, that is the easiest pathway to love, which in turn will lead to improved business results.

Yes, being intentionally decent and showing minimal civility towards others will help you be *more successful in the workplace*. I haven't forgotten you, Overworked Businessperson!

Back to our beleaguered hotel restaurant staff. Their consensus is that if the previous manager, Jane (not her real name), had called and asked them to work a double on Mother's Day, they would do it, because they wanted to do it for Jane. "Jane started from a place of generosity, and you knew she had your back," one staff member recalled. "Which unlocked a whole dimension of support from us that wouldn't have been there if she had arrived from a place of scarcity. I would've done it for Jane, but I'm not doing it now."

Look at the undercurrents of this hotel restaurant situation in terms of scarcity versus generosity (and in this context, generosity is synonymous with love). Fundamentally, many toxic behaviors are rooted in the perpetrator's feeling and fear of scarcity. They think they have to exert unyielding control in order to motivate people. They think that if they're not harsh with others, if they ever give an inch, if they don't lay down the law and keep people frightened, awed, or shamed into submission, then they'll be taken advantage of. But it's actually the reverse. When you create a feeling of scarcity in others through being a bully and a tyrant, you inevitably rob yourself of your team's best efforts. Because no one can do their best work for someone who makes them feel like crap.

In contrast, when you treat your team members with basic decency—a greeting when they arrive at work, eye contact when you encounter them, a brief acknowledgment for what they're doing—they will dig deeper, commit longer, and try *so much harder*. Because when you start by demonstrating that you noticed the fact that they showed up for work at all, then they will reciprocate in kind by giving a damn about doing what matters to you. It's not magical thinking. It's consistent with human nature.

If you just had a knee-jerk reaction of "but if I'm nice all the time, if I thank people just for walking in the door, if I'm generous with people—they'll take advantage of my weakness! And nobody respects a doormat!" then you are having human fears that you'll be preyed upon like the slow gazelle in a herd. But take heart. First of all, I'm not for a moment suggesting that you should be a doormat of naïve amiability in a way that makes you susceptible to being taken advantage of. (For skills in setting boundaries around your generosity and using it with business savvy, see chapter 8 on accountability.)

Here's the key: Generosity is not weakness. Generosity is the often-unused code to opening up everyone's capacity to contribute above and beyond what is asked of them. If you don't tap into that wellspring of potential effort, you are leaving money on the table in terms of goodwill, energy, and productivity (all of which translate into literal money as well).

Consider a reflection from longtime TV producer Lis Rowinski: "I remember when I was an assistant, and my boss would get calls from Jeff Robinov, when he was the president of production at Warner Bros. Jeff's assistant was named Felicia, and maybe she was feeding him my name before I answered the phone—but Jeff would greet me by name, even though I was just an assistant connecting a phone call to my boss. I would do anything for Jeff Robinov if he called me today, because he was kind to me and said hello to me by name. It made me feel like I had some sort of place. I think about that a lot." In her own high-powered life now, Lis learns the names of every assistant she talks with and consistently greets them by name when she makes a phone call to their office.

The takeaway is *when you exercise rudimentary courtesy in acknowledging the existence of the person you're interacting with, the rewards are truly exponential.*

⊕

But what about going beyond saying hello to everyone when they arrive at work? (And if you're not doing that, please start, with my gratitude on behalf of your team members.) Here's an effective pathway to truly elevated business outcomes.

First, *teach yourself to love the sea* (going back to the quote that begins this chapter). In other words, teach yourself to genuinely love the work you're engaged in.

Does the work not present itself as lovable? Totally get it. But even in a tough environment or with few emotional payoffs, the invitation here is to *find what there is to love* in your difficult field. It doesn't have to be an aspect like prestige, money, or intellectual satisfaction. But ideally, it's something connected to the larger goals of the work, the people you reach, and the end results of the endeavor. Find what is worthwhile and meaningful in the work itself and remind yourself of that every day. It might help to create a physical touchstone that you can put in a visible place for a quick reset of your perspective every time you feel discouraged, annoyed, or disconnected at work. This touchstone can remind you of what's important and valuable to you about the job you're in, and it can help you hold onto those things when small frustrations start to pile up (as they will).

Then, *show respect for the work.* Speak and act respectfully about your work in front of your colleagues and in public. (This one shift will change your entire environment, by the way.)

Meaning: Embrace the work and do it to the best of your ability, without holding back emotional or mental commitment to it. Take your work seriously and keep your outward demeanor positive and supportive of the team's goals—even if it's not a job you intend to stay in for the long term. Even if it's not a job you particularly enjoy. Even if it's a job where you legitimately believe you could do your boss's job better than they are doing it. Those things may all be true, but if you let your personal frustrations bleed out into how you engage with your daily tasks, what you'll actually be doing is showing others that you are *not* suited to lead. An upright leader can be dissatisfied with their current situation while still demonstrating the utmost respect for the work itself.

Then, do your best to *create joy for yourself as a result of doing this work—especially* if it's a job you haven't found to be pleasant before now.

This one might be a challenge, and I'm not discounting the stresses and obstacles that are intertwined with many jobs. But you may be surprised how much more satisfaction and enjoyment you can find in your job if you can get into the habit of appreciating the process itself, and if you can expand your view of your job to include not just the tasks you get paid for but also the people you interact with, the environments you're introduced to, and the quiet details and broad ambitions of what your work requires. As a friend of mine puts it, there's great beauty in the desert, if only we pause long enough to look around and notice it.

After you've learned to love this sea, bring others into that same love. A crucial part of this is *finding what there is to admire, value, and even be fond of in your team members.*

Not to compare the people around you to a desert, but let's take a (hopefully hypothetical) worst-case scenario where you have a low opinion of your colleagues. What if you pause to look around at them and notice their individual interests and life experiences? Another friend of mine has gone so far as to institute a monthly lunchtime tradition in her corporate department, where everyone takes turns giving a thirty-minute, workplace-appropriate talk on a subject near and dear to their heart. Topics have covered every possible hobby and a wide range of personal passions, including pop culture fandom. Team members now look forward to these opportunities to learn more about each other and about these engagingly varied topics, and the entire department has bonded over these talks.

This brings me to the second aspect of bringing others into your love of the sea, and it's equally crucial: *Show respect for your team members.*

Meaning: Speak graciously about them—not just to their faces but when they're out of earshot too. And this includes how you speak about them via text, email, and social media. I am indeed suggesting that people *lay off the snarky comments, period.*

I know that might be a bummer for some. But the title of this book isn't *Lead with Kindness: You Still Get to be Petty!*

Although it might be an adjustment to say only polite and professional things about your coworkers, you will find in the end that it's a time and energy saver. Because you'll never have to worry about something you said getting back to the wrong person, and also people will come to realize that they can trust you not to be two-faced. This one area of restraint—keeping your comments about your colleagues civil and respectful no matter what, no matter who you're communicating with—can totally shift the dynamic of a workplace, because your team will witness and follow your lead. (Meanwhile, I guarantee you that if you trash-talk others, your team will follow your lead there as well.)

As you connect with your team members on an authentic level, and as you show them that you truly respect them as individual human beings, you will find it much easier to *create joy when all of you engage in the work at hand.* And you'll have a much easier time leading them to share your love of the sea where all of you have found yourselves together, building ships.

This might not be simple or easy, so I encourage you to look at it as a process. If you keep at it over time, those incremental and even intermittent improvements, steadied into habit, will gradually transform how you show up for other people and how they show up for you.

So, quick regroup on how to generate love as a force for producing better outcomes:

1. Acknowledge team members every time you encounter them.
2. Show respect for the work you're engaged in.
3. Find what there is to admire in your team members, and keep that admiration front of mind. It'll show forth in your demeanor, and it *will* improve the team dynamic.

Change rarely happens overnight. But change can happen, and it has a much higher chance of happening when you step forward and set things—and love—in motion.

Executive Highlights: Love

I'm too earnest to write a cheeky preamble to a recap about love. Remember the following:

Snack-sized takeaway: Love is not weakness. Love is an engine for productivity when that love comes from fostering supportive community, expressing respect for people's work, acknowledging your colleagues' existence as individuals, and articulating a sense of possibility about the intended outcomes.

Business benefit: Love for a common goal is a much stronger and more lasting motivator than money, advancement, or credit. When a team feels meaningfully connected to a shared goal, they'll work hard for it, and they'll do so even in challenging conditions.

Sustainable strategy: Catch people being good. In other words, notice when someone is making a contribution, and express appreciation for that contribution even if—especially if—it's part of their everyday duties. By doing this, you'll show respect for your colleague's function on the team. You'll also normalize their experience of having a positive interaction with you. And your example will help create a culture where team members consistently encourage each other.

Seriously, try this at home: Soothe your own nervous system so that you can show love to others. To soothe yourself, recreate a treat from childhood (a favorite of mine is snacking on graham crackers dipped in milk while reading a few pages from *The Lord of the Rings*; the window to my psyche is opening). When your own nervous system gets calmed and reassured, that will generate an increased ability to demonstrate love for those around you.

Even if you're not the boss yet: Ask for help with a task, and then actually leave the task in your colleague's hands. Meaning: Really trust your colleague instead of micromanaging or second-guessing them. Empower them with these words: "I trust your judgment." When your colleague feels your trust and sees that you believe in their ability to produce results, that will increase their love of the sea you're sailing together.

To lead with love, you'll have to expand your tolerance for the discomfort of *coming from a place of sincere goodwill for other people, even those who irritate and disappoint you.* I never said this would be easy. But the habit does grow with practice.

But wait, there's more: Now that you've taught yourself and others to love the sea you're in, it's time to build on that love, empowered by the inclusion, kindness, and trust you've been fostering as well. It's time to add the superpower of *sustaining internal calm.* In the next chapter you'll find out how an intentional sense of calm will not slow you down—on the contrary, it will lead you to break through impasses and achiever greater success than ever. Read on....

CHAPTER 5

CALM BREEDS SUCCESS

"Every day is a complete mess. One
crisis after another. And at the end
of every day, we go over the rapids
into the next day with zero plan!
And the whole thing starts again."

*—An anonymous professional who works for
a highly paid leader at a prestigious job*

"Oh yes, and this too."

—Jack Kornfield, Buddhist mindfulness teacher

I almost made this chapter the first chapter of the book, because I feel that calm is the essential tenet from which everything else flows better. But I wanted to match the structure of my podcast, and, also, you can use all of the tactics in this book without being calm—but it all works so much better if you're calm.

In this context, calm is not a synonym for being passively *relaxed* or even feeling good. Instead:

**Calm is the active skill of
maintaining internal stability
despite surrounding chaos.**

So I'm talking about the kind of calm that allows you to focus, be present, be professional, and be effective—even while you're operating on no sleep, your aging mother is querulously demanding that you pick her up from the hospital, your soon-to-be-ex-spouse is sending you a string of text messages about your divorce proceedings, your higher-ups have raised labor-intensive requests concerning the project your team has worked on for weeks, you're juggling bills and childcare duties, and it's stiflingly hot in the makeshift garage office where you're leading a Zoom meeting during a global pandemic while hundreds of people are waiting for your update about when they'll be able to go back to work in another country, which is dependent on shifting government policies and evolving union agreements totally beyond your control. (This might or might not have been me on a summer afternoon in 2020.)

And yet, despite surrounding chaos, it is absolutely possible to develop muscles to re-center yourself in meaningful purpose, ground yourself in a larger perspective, and still your mind to discern among the choices before you. Even better, as you strengthen these muscles and build this mental discipline, you will find that you are able to return to this state of focused presence more and more quickly each time you need to. And your focused presence will empower you to be a more effective and successful leader while also maintaining a professional outward demeanor. In short, these practices will make you more of a badass, and as a bonus you'll even look like one.

Sound helpful? Great. Let's get there together.

The tools in this chapter are designed to sustain your own composure and the composure of others. You can't control circumstances, but you can control how you choose to respond to circumstances. You are generating calm so that your heart—coming from the place of your best self—is free to choose how to act in the midst of difficult circumstances. Yes, you look more put together when you're calm, and you can more easily be pleasant. But it's also a precursor to productivity and therefore profit, Overworked Businessperson.

Here's what proved it to me. As part of the launch of the *Nancy Drew* writers' room in season one, I invited meditation teacher Dr. Christiane Wolf to lead a workshop on mindfulness because I wanted to provide my team members with tools to manage their own anxiety (as a segment of society, writers are a jittery bunch). From my own experience, I believed mindfulness would improve their lives; and in my enlightened self-interest, I correctly anticipated that calmer writers would be better able to contribute to the conversational and creative flow of our daily story sessions in the room. For most of season one, the mindfulness techniques we learned were simply a nurturing keepsake from those first onboarding days. And then 2020 came and COVID-19 happened.

We shut down physical production, sent all our crew members home halfway through the day on Friday, March 13, and resumed work in the writers' room the following Monday on a mysterious online platform—new to all of us—called Zoom. This was at a juncture when people were hoarding toilet paper, when the public didn't know about face masks, and when a vaccine was nowhere in sight. In short, everyone was freaking out. And I knew if we didn't find a way to get centered, the overwhelming worries of the COVID-19 pandemic would take the group's conversations down a bottomless rabbit hole that would make us feel even worse and, not inconsequentially, prevent us from doing any actual work.

So that very first Monday morning on Zoom, I started a new daily practice: After allowing about five minutes for housekeeping announcements and a general acknowledgment of how messed-up the world was, we all turned off our Zoom cameras and listened to a three-minute breathing meditation from Dr. Christiane Wolf's SoundCloud recordings. When the little bell rang at the end of her very soothing guided meditation, that meant it was time to begin work. This morning meditation persisted for every season that followed, even when we went back to in-person meetings, and it was a key to our efficient, high-performing, and sane writers' room.

Exercising calm has obvious positive effects on workflow, such as increased clarity and sensible decision-making. But the true business benefit is that when you are a calm leader, it's so much easier for people to tolerate and maybe even enjoy your presence. End result: Team members want to stay instead of leave. So by promoting a culture of calm—by managing your own emotions, encouraging mindfulness, and implementing a humane pace every day—you will improve employee retention, which saves you money, and you'll generate sustainable productivity, which makes you money. I think it's a bonus that people feel better when they're calm, but even if you don't like it when people around you feel better, remember this:

**Fostering your team's
calm is a shrewd tactic to
increase profitability.**

Another metric that shows the positive impact of calm comes from the world of law enforcement. Police training in de-escalation gives officers valuable tools for navigating and defusing potentially harmful encounters. Methods include shifting body language to convey openness instead of confrontation, speaking quietly and in a measured tone, listening actively and empathetically, and offering choices and reassurance instead of threats. The success of this behavior shift has been measured in lower injury rates for both police personnel and the individuals they engage with, fewer complaints from the public, and increased success in the peaceful resolution of situations.

In other words, manifesting calm can save taxpayers tens of millions of dollars by preventing violence, lawsuits, and claims for damages. Once again, a kindness-driven principle results in a crucial, far-reaching, and cost-saving benefit.

My theory on why leaders don't address chaos in their workplace is that those individuals are emotionally addicted to what they get out of that chaos. If there's no center, then the leader has to be the person to make all the decisions. If there's no plan, nobody can point to a plan that's not being carried out. If there are constant fires to put out, the leader never has to look at the bigger things that they are failing at—such as time management, clear communication, decision-making, and uncomfortable conversations. These are all activities that would make them perhaps not be liked immediately or all the time.

But if that conflict avoidance and emotional addiction are what governs you, then know this: What people *actually* like is when you keep your act together and don't make everyone exist in a whirling ball of mayhem.

If you just had a knee-jerk reaction of "but it's not my fault that the mayhem exists! You have no idea the number of people I answer to/the amount of crap I get bombarded with/the constant fires I have to put out! Who will get things done if I'm sitting around listening to guided meditations? Don't I need to keep running headfirst at all of this stuff with maximum adrenaline in order to lead effectively?" then you are definitely a human who's in a stressful environment, and you really need to slow down and give yourself the gift of calm.

Deep breath: You'll be better at putting out fires, you'll be better at getting things done, and you'll lead more effectively without the kind of adrenaline that comes from plunging over the rapids by first regaining your equanimity.

And if you can't get yourself to a neutral state right away, *imagine* how you would respond if you did not feel emotionally attached to the situation, and then act accordingly. You will be surprised at how effective it is to *act as a calm person would*.

"How the heck am I supposed to do that? I don't actually know what calm people do!" you might retort while pacing around and squeezing a stress ball. Fortunately for us, there are people whose literal job is to foster calm in others. Let's learn from how these professionals calm agitated clients in high-stakes situations.

Case Study: Conflict Mediation as a Tool for Stabilizing People (Including You)

Eyal Rabinovitch is cofounder and co-CEO of Resetting the Table (RTT), a nonprofit organization that trains leaders to bridge and transform toxic divides. A core part of their framework is teaching skills for healthy engagement between people who have opposing viewpoints. In the abstract, what they're doing is providing practical and tested tools for conflict mediation: listening without judgment, asking questions that get at underlying concerns, and building constructive dialogue. These problem-solving tactics are applicable to all walks of life, including business. Through these tactics, people's defensiveness gets disarmed, and their reactivity gets replaced by a much calmer openness to new ideas and perspectives.

On the ground, RTT's work brings together people who have diametrically opposed political and personal beliefs in a way that helps them find mutual understanding, civility, and openness to learning about each other's stances in the world and even collaborating to address shared problems. Importantly, understanding does *not* have to mean agreement. But it does mean that people come away with skills to depolarize fraught conversations and break through emotional impasses.

"None of this sounds relaxing!" you chime in. True, but the goal here is not to relax. The goal is to find ways to maintain your own internal stability during stressful situations, and conflict mediation is actually all about *stabilizing* the people involved. Stability is a first step to negotiating disagreements. In other words, mediators calm people so that they can move forward—and that kind of calm and forward motion is what enables us to perform and succeed at work.

When I spoke with Rabinovitch, I asked how he uses mediation skills as a superpower to stabilize people, so their emotions don't get in the way of achieving their desired outcomes. (As with all the other principles in this book, *calm is a pathway to your desired outcomes*—just to remind you of what's in it for you.)

Put another way, I wanted to know how to course correct when we get emotionally and psychologically destabilized by circumstances. Destabilization is what you experience when events spin out of your control, you experience a disappointment, someone breaks your trust, or anything goes wrong in your life. Destabilization is the opposite of calm, and our unthinking reactions to feeling destabilized cause many ills in the workplace and the world.

"From my vantage point, a lot of being thrown off…center is what happens when people feel they are not accurately seen or fully seen," Rabinovitch said, adding that people will go to great lengths in their attempts to be seen how they want to be seen in the world. (Social media has plenty of evidence of this.) "One thing that people don't consider very often is this need to be seen the way we want to be seen and understood the way we want to be understood. People are deeply invested in others' perceptions of them, and that becomes foundational to their sense that *things are as they should be.*"

That basic sense that things are as they should be, that everything is okay in the world—our underlying feeling of calm—gets fractured when we believe we're not being seen accurately, we're being made invisible by others, or we're being misunderstood. The barrier to productive engagement is especially high when the atmosphere is charged, people are carrying wounds from the past, or the environment is toxic.

When those circumstances collide, then the resulting tension, resentment, and emotional disconnect leads not only to polarization within groups, but it also leads to people getting stuck in their feelings of being destabilized. Destabilized people have a hard time taking in each other's viewpoints, and consequently, they have difficulty working together and achieving their goals.

RTT uses the language of *stability* rather than calmness, because you can be stable in your mindset while also being animated and demonstrative, which might be contrasted with the typical perception of calm. RTT's methods aim to ensure that people are seen the way they wish to be seen and known the way they wish to be known. This helps people get centered and stable, so that they reach a position where they can take other people's viewpoints in and express their own voices to say what they have to say. Once that happens for all parties in a conversation, they can talk about things they couldn't talk about before. This kind of stability and calm receptivity leads to more productive work environments.

In order to invest in the receptivity of someone else, you draw out the meaning of what they're sitting with and give it recognition. Take the time to demonstrate that you see the lens, the self-understanding, the conceptual frame that the other person holds. This *isn't* the same as agreeing with the other person on any of the above. But when you can articulate an understanding of the other person in a way that prompts them to say, "Yes, that's exactly me"—that opens a lot of doors.

"We do it so infrequently to each other, give each other this kind of recognition in our culture—it gives a sense of 'this person has taken the time to truly understand my lens'—that it makes harder conversations more likely to be successful," said Rabinovitch. "The more you see the layers and what's behind each successive layer, the more the stability and trust grow, and that's how we get through the hard stuff together."

When you directly and respectfully engage with difficult disconnects and charged conversations, Rabinovitch said, the rewards are tremendous and long-lasting: "When you can hear each other out, and get through it and say look what we just did together, and then that trust is built—you say to yourself...*we can walk through the fire together.*"

⊕

Great news, restoring calm while having difficult conversations—and creating internal stability in the process, so you can get to a shared goal on the other side—is something you can learn to do at home (and at work). The methodology of RTT is grounded in three techniques:

- following meaning
- demonstrating understanding, and
- naming differences.

The end result of applying these techniques is that you will be better able to move the needle with the person you need to supervise/reach agreement with/enlist to your cause. Here's how to put the techniques to use towards your goals.

Following meaning: When you follow (instead of lead, for this moment!) as a communicator, you put a temporary pause button on your own agenda. This means: For the first part of the interaction, you set aside what *you're* interested in, concerned about, and curious about. All of that needs to wait until later, because when you have your own agenda and concerns in the front of your mind, you have a human tendency to guess at what's going on for the other person. More often than not, our guesses will be inaccurate, and our instinct to jump to conclusions and fill in the blanks for the other person will get in the way of them telling us what's *actually* important to them.

So instead of giving in to the temptation to skip to the part where we explain why we're right, we neutrally investigate the other person's terrain, so we can start to see the situation through their lens. RTT suggests investigating by asking respectful questions about "signposts," such as repeated words, emotional intensity, and unusual turns of phrase. For instance, an agitated team member might tell you: "I don't want to get dragged into that extra project. I'm already getting dragged into doing all these other extra tasks, and no one notices that they're grinding me into dust!"

In this example, let's say your own agenda is to convince this team member to take on the extra project. Your unsubstantiated guess is that they're simply unwilling to work as hard as you need them to, and your own frustration makes you want to insist that they complete the assignment with some version of "because I said so."

But what if you put your own agenda, guesses, and frustration on the back burner for a few minutes while you *ask questions about what's important to the other person*? You would respectfully and neutrally ask them why it's feeling like they get dragged into things, ask them to share more about the energy behind their comments, and ask them to bring you into their experience of getting ground into dust.

You'll be surprised what layers get unearthed when you *follow* the other person in conversation to where they want to go, as opposed to correcting them, filling in the gaps for them about what they're trying to express, or trying to get your viewpoint equally heard (at this stage).

In the above scenario, you could find out that the person has only been in their position for a couple of months; they were promoted to that department because of a specific skill set, and the extra project you want them to take on has nothing to do with the skills for which they were promoted. You could find out that the intensity of their pushback is coming not from laziness but from anxiety that they'll underperform in the original aspects of their job. Good thing you didn't jump to conclusions without inviting them to share their perspective!

Demonstrating understanding: This next part is simpler. After listening for signposts and asking questions about what's going on for the other person, you articulate your new awareness about what you've just learned. You want to make sure you understand the other person fully and accurately, so they can get to a place where they say, "Yes, that's exactly right. That's what I'm experiencing; that's where I'm coming from." This doesn't have to take a lot of time, but people rarely bother to do it.

While exploring whether your understanding is accurate, RTT recommends using "you" statements, such as "It sounds like you're experiencing these assignments as a weight, and that's frustrating to you because you haven't yet had time to adjust to your new position in the department. You're worried that if you take on one more project, you won't be able to excel in the area you were actually promoted for, because instead you're getting ground into dust with these other projects that aren't even in your original wheelhouse. Is that right?"

In this example, I've added a layer where, through asking authentic questions, you discovered the deeper fears and drives underneath what could have been misinterpreted as petulance or even lack of ambition. When you don't take time to find out what's really going on for other people—when you guess at their motivations, assume what their perspective is, and fill in the blanks about them in a way that's unfair or inaccurate—that's very destabilizing to those around you, and yet it's something we do to each other constantly.

But when you show other people that you see them as they wish to be seen and understand them as they wish to be understood, you help them get back to internal stability. That internal stability, that calm, will make all sorts of other things (receptivity, connection, change, collaboration, growth, or taking on that extra assignment for you) much more possible.

Naming differences: This third technique is exactly what it sounds like. Having gotten an accurate understanding of the other person as they wish to be understood (in this case, a new team member wants to be seen as a conscientious high achiever, but feels that side projects are preventing them from proving their worth in their area of expertise), you then articulate some differences between what the other person is seeing and what you're seeing.

Continuing with our example, you might say to this team member, "You and I have a difference about how we see this additional project. You see it as a distraction from what you were hired to do, something that decreases what you can contribute because it will take extra time. I see this project as an expansion of your value here, especially because the skills you learn from this project will be ones you can use in your new department going forward."

It's important to be honest and direct about this assessment of differences. It might be tempting to minimize the differences in perspectives, but that's actually counter to your end goal of acknowledging where people are really coming from, neutralizing the charge from these differences, and making it possible to productively address them. "You see this extra project as unnecessary busywork, is that correct? But I see it as something that's important to our long-term business development."

Once everyone agrees that the differences have been accurately named, then you can move towards bridging the gap between viewpoints. Ask questions to deepen everyone's understanding of the differences. Then shift the conversation with the benefit of this new clarity, with people speaking directly to the heart of the matter and hopefully connecting better because they can now see the reasonable underpinnings of various viewpoints. Importantly, just because the parties *understand* each other doesn't mean they have to *agree* with each other. But at least they're coming from a place of basic mutual respect and accuracy of perception. (How often is that absent from the orbits we travel in and witness?)

In this example, you've gained an insight into how this team member's vocalized frustration is actually coming from a desire to perform better in their specialty, and not from a desire to do less work. And the team member has learned that you've actually assigned them this extra project out of a desire to increase their value to the company, not diminish it.

With the improved internal stability for both sides with these discoveries, now you can continue the conversation about the project with an increased sense of calm and therefore receptivity to further discussion about *your* agenda. So, for you Overworked Businesspeople out there, calming people down can directly lead to you getting what you want from them.

**Increased stability leads
to improved connection
and receptivity, which
leads to better results.**

Quick regroup on strategies to restore and sustain calm:

By using mediation techniques like those developed by RTT, you can stabilize the internal states of team members who are struggling to collaborate or even communicate in the midst of work stress and other chaotic circumstances:

1. Ask questions about what's important to the other person, not about what's important to you.
2. Tell the other person what you've come to understand about their perspective. Understanding another person's point of view does not have to equal agreeing with it. Explore until they let you know you're seeing them as they wish to be seen.
3. To create even more receptivity in the other person and set the stage to productively address differences, name the differences between their viewpoint and yours. This is part of acknowledging how they wish to be seen and takes the sting out of differences.
4. Establishing this new level of understanding will help the other person get to a place of internal stability so that you can then (finally, I know) tell them what you need them to hear, with a much higher likelihood that they'll be able to calmly and productively take in your perspective.

After you've stabilized everyone's internal states, including your own, and defused the charge of differences, you can find more success in moving forward as a group.

Now that we've investigated the external management of calm, let's talk about the internal management of calm, also known as mindfulness.

⊕

I find work to be a very soothing pastime. This probably comes from a childhood of being constantly pushed to achieve in order to win my parents' approval; for me, being busily occupied with a task leads to feelings of increased calm, because some part of my reptilian/childhood brain locks into the familiar pursuit of an emotional reward.

And there's another reason I feel calm when I'm working: It's the fact that I'm concentrating on something outside of myself. Mindfulness meditation teacher Dr. Christiane Wolf showed my writing staff the classic exercise where she hands you a single raisin and tells you to experience this raisin with all five of your senses. Meaning: Roll it around on your skin, feel its slight stickiness and the firmness of its ridges. Smell its sugary tang. Closely examine its wrinkles and colors as you hold it up to the light. Listen to it (yes, listen to the raisin) when you hold it next to your ear and gently squish it and move it around. Finally, put it onto your tongue, feel its wrinkles and texture while your saliva collects around it, and then very slowly and deliberately chew it between your teeth in a burst of mellow sweetness, turning it in your mouth while it breaks apart into smaller and smaller gooey pieces, which you finally swallow.

The more you focus on the raisin in this exercise, the more you will get the point, which is that it's difficult to truly focus on more than one thing at a time. It's certainly possible to experience many things in rapid succession—thoughts, feelings, physical sensations—but when you slow your attention to be fully present for exactly one thing at a time, you'll find that this ramp-down of your processing speed will help you move towards calm.

"But what does any of this have to do with making money?" Overworked Businessperson shouts through the doorway of our meditation room.

Well, I'll tell you. Sustaining calm in yourself and others is a business benefit because

- calm people can make better decisions,
- calm people can act professionally towards those around them, and
- calm people can manage the process instead of getting overrun by it.

Before I continue on to a fuller examination of these truths, as well as strategies to generate your own internal calm, here's an important clarification:

Calm is not the magical absence of stress. *Calm is not a passive state.*

Instead—*calm is produced by intentional actions,* namely

- re-centering yourself in the present moment, and
- maintaining the discipline to operate at the level of your best self.

Take a deep breath, please, and get your body and your mind in the same place for what's next.

Okay. Being present and centered and operating from the level of your best self allows you to sustain a healthy boundary between you and your circumstance. After you have that healthy boundary between who you are and what your circumstance is, *then* you'll be able to choose a mindful response to that circumstance.

Without being centered in your best self, without creating that boundary, you will be much more likely to get lost in the vortex of whatever problem may be at hand and much more likely to be *reacting* to stress instead of *managing* it.

And we are in the business of management, after all. To get back to why calm is a business benefit, let me break it down for you even further, Overworked Businessperson:

Calm people can make better decisions:

- decisions about how to use resources (saving time and using money wisely).
- decisions about how to balance short-term gains against long-term planning and vision (keeping the big picture in mind, which increases chances of earning more money).
- decisions about how to keep people safe (preventing injuries, reducing time off from work due to stress, avoiding lawsuits, and therefore saving money).

Calm people can act professionally towards those around them:

- This reduces HR complaints and lawsuits (saving time and saving money).
- It improves team morale, longevity, and focus (optimizing time spent at work and making more money).
- It fosters an environment where people feel safer to do their best work (which equals more money).

Calm people can manage the process instead of getting overrun by it, because of:

- the ability to receive and respond to ongoing input from multiple sources instead of getting overwhelmed and shutting down emotionally and ignoring phone calls, emails, and texts; bottlenecks waste time and money

- carving out time to plan ahead, forecast, and communicate with the team so that you can strategize about both saving and making money

- setting and maintaining boundaries for workflow and energy so that you don't get stuck in a loop of diminishing returns where you're constantly behind, playing catch-up, and putting out the fires in front of you—instead of engaging with the team's (money-saving and money-making) goals at a high and holistic level

When you set out to get all of the above accomplished, another underlying principle is this: This works better when you are present *as your best self.*

Being your best self is the secret sauce of calm. Also, great news and a surprising twist: The process of becoming present as your best self…can be fun.

Whew! Stepping back from managerial environments, let's loosen up our brains a little bit. Imagine a time when you were really happy. Really alive. Only focused on the awesome thing that you were experiencing—just for that instant. That's being present.

Notice when you are experiencing life as the best version of yourself. Store that memory carefully, so that you can recreate and relive it very specifically and vividly in your mind, even for just a moment. Because that moment is what you'll use to remind yourself of what it feels like to be living as the most admirable and worthy version of yourself.

This is my extrapolation of what's known as Buddha nature. It's the most evolved part of you: your fundamental potential to act wisely and compassionately. It's the truest part of your identity where you experience joy, connection, and a perspective beyond your everyday human limitations. Buddha nature is pretty awesome, and I believe that all humans possess it, even you, Overworked Businessperson. It's just a matter of stilling your mind enough to remember it and tap into its inner stability.

So imagine that your Buddha nature is deep within you as your absolute core best self. And then recognize that the stressful things in your current circumstance—a crisis at work, an argument with your partner, a professional setback, a health challenge for a loved one, the general state of the world—those are things that are happening *outside* of you. Those circumstances are not who you are, so, as Buddhist teacher Jack Kornfield advises:

Don't let outside circumstances colonize your heart.

How can you avoid letting circumstances colonize your heart?

1. Come up with a vivid sense memory of being your best self—that moment of being centered and present and alive in something that truly fulfilled you—and develop the reflex of quickly tapping into that sense memory the next time something stressful happens.
2. Remember that you are your best self, and you're in one physical and emotional spot over here (I'm putting one hand on my heart while typing with my other hand) while the circumstance you've encountered is outside of

you, separate from you, and in an entirely different spot over there (I'm pointing to my right).

Example: If you're driving and someone cuts you off in traffic, instead of thinking angry thoughts about the other driver, tap into your memory of your best self, and reexperience the feeling of how that best version of you is who you really are. After that, say to yourself: "I'm over here [maybe putting a hand on your heart]—I am my best self. Oh yes, and this too—[pointing to your right]—someone just cut me off in traffic. Oh yes, and this too." The more you build this muscle, the more you can use it to calm yourself and sustain internal stability whenever challenges come your way.

And for those of us who don't always have time to go through a sense memory exercise in the course of a busy day, here's advice from Cathy Salser from A Window Between Worlds: During your calm moments, you can make lists of tactics to get yourself back into your "resilience zone," which is where we exist when things are basically going okay and we are not at our wits' end. Then, the next time you get pushed out of your resilience zone by stress, conflict, and other challenges, you have a ready-made list of helpful tactics to refer to, and you can use those tactics to get yourself back into your sweet spot of internal stability.

A tactic on your list might be physiological (for instance, box breathing, where you inhale for a count of four, hold your breath for a count of four, exhale for a count of four, and pause for a count of four before inhaling again). It could be a specific peaceful memory that you visualize because you know it soothes your nerves. It could be a meaningful phrase that helps you remember your capacity to handle challenges. Whatever your touchstones are, you'll do better to have them quickly accessible in a handy list (literally posted on your phone/computer/desk), as opposed to defaulting into an autopilot spiral of reactivity when stressful situations arise.

Along with your list of self-calming tactics, when you get activated by circumstances and chaos, continuously redirect negative and stressful thoughts into focusing on what is good in your life (and in the world) and focusing on what you can control. Keep yourself away from the rabbit hole of negative thoughts and impulsive reactions, so that you don't lose yourself inside someone else's stress, displeasure, sadness, or frustration. When you notice yourself descending into your own spiral or getting pulled off course into someone else's vortex, don't waste time and energy beating yourself up for spiraling. Just flag it ("Oh, I'm spiraling again. I got pulled into someone else's vortex again") and immediately restart the centering process.

I told you calm was an active thing. It's also a continuous process. This is simple but not easy, to quote Dr. Christiane Wolf.

So I'll use this moment to take my own advice, and here are some touchstones from my own list of self-calming tactics:

- Gratitude! This is crucial. I did a little bit of online shopping while taking a break from writing this chapter and bought a pretty set of thank-you notes for a group of people who are taking part in a public service event with me next week. It cheered me up to think of specifically thanking each one of them and expressing my deep appreciation for their generosity of time and resources. Mind you, gratitude doesn't have to involve internet shopping. Thanking people can always be done for free, and you will accrue good energy in the process.

- Meaningful phrase: When facing an impending deadline, I sometimes tell myself: "Bird by bird." This advice is from Anne Lamott's insightful book of the same name. In sharing her learning curve as an anxious writer and human, Lamott tells the story of her younger brother who had neglected an important school project until the night before the deadline and was now confronted by the overwhelming task of cataloging a seemingly endless list of wildlife birds in the remaining hours before the assignment was due. Lamott's dad sat down next to her brother, and, in answer to the boy's tearful question about how he could possibly get it all done in time, her dad's steadying response was "we'll take it bird by bird." And they did.

- Engage with something bigger than yourself: I'll expand on this topic in chapter 10 on service. But the headline is that being of service to others can give you valuable perspective, get you out of your own head, and remind you of your purpose in the world—all of which will help re-center you.

- Mindfulness meditation: There are many free resources online for this, including the Zoom meditation workshop recording I helped organize with Dr. Christiane Wolf in the wake of the LA wildfires. You can find the recording on my Instagram @melindahsuLA.

- The classic 5-4-3-2-1 technique, which is a go-to recommended by my older son Casey: name five things you can see, four things you can touch, three things you can hear, two things you can smell, and one thing you can taste. This will get you centered in the present moment, which is the only moment you can actually affect.

- Make things with your hands: Any kind of creative moment can be centering (even doodling on a Post-it while you're on a phone call), but if you have a few extra minutes to get back in touch with your childhood self through a tactile experience like folding a paper airplane or squishing a lump of Silly Putty, the physical sensations themselves can be very calming.

- Carve out windows of time when you are not looking at a screen: Work with a pen and paper in a room without electronics for half an hour, spend time outside without your phone, or have a conversation with a trusted friend whose energy will not drain yours. Downtime is crucial to calm—a matter of quality versus quantity (though quantity is great if you can get it).

- Make sure you are adequately hydrated and your blood sugar is stable: Carrying a reusable water bottle and keeping nonperishable snacks within arm's reach can be lifesavers for your focus, energy level, and mood. (When I joined the staff of *The Vampire Diaries*, my new colleagues noticed my daily mood growing hangrier and hangrier as lunchtime approached. As a result, whenever they heard my voice's late-morning tone get a little sharper, they adopted the practice of jokingly reminding me that it was time to eat a snack. After about a week of this, I began to preemptively have a healthy mid-morning snack to steady my blood sugar, and my professional life has been better ever since.)

These are strategies I shared with my former writers' rooms during the Writers Guild strike of 2023, when all of us walked the picket lines in total uncertainty for nearly six income-less months. I told them at the beginning of the strike that one of their primary goals needed to be *sustaining internal calm* in order to stay centered, sane, and functional amid destabilizing and debilitating circumstances. I reminded them that the one thing they could control at this time was how they managed their own responses to the stress around them. I believe it helped all of us get through an extraordinarily challenging stretch of time, and I hope it helps you in your daily life as well.

Executive Highlights: Calm

This is for those of you who had to step away and make the world turn instead of reading the earlier part of this chapter.

Snack-sized takeaway: By training yourself to remain calm and sustain internal stability in any situation, you will super-charge every other skill you have, including your ability to bring out the best in your team.

Business benefit: Calm leaders see more clearly, act more effectively, and get better long-term results than people who run around with their hair on fire. Plus, a consistently calm demeanor is genuinely mystifying to most people, which gives you an advantage in your interactions with the great majority of the population.

Sustainable strategy: Use "straw breaths" to slow down your physiological response to stress. Breathe in while counting silently, then breathe out for double that count. Example: inhale (one), exhale (one…two). Inhale (one, two), exhale (one…two…three… four). Bonus: This can be done entirely surreptitiously, especially on Zoom, so that you can be calming and re-centering yourself in the middle of any circumstance, without anyone ever noticing.

Seriously, try this at home: Practice building in a pause before you respond to something. During that pause (count to three in your head), picture a green balloon quickly deflating. The balloon represents you releasing your emotional attachment to whatever just happened. This will help you respond from a place of detachment, instead of heat, stress, or reactivity.

Even if you're not the boss yet: Stay centered in what you stand for, in the passions of your heart, and intentionally operate from that place—*because* it is needed. Do your work because it's your reason for being on the planet. This will help you sustain inner peace, for real.

To lead with calm, you'll have to expand your tolerance for the discomfort of *maintaining internal stability in the midst of situations that are beyond your control.* The world needs your internal stability, so that you can see circumstances clearly—without allowing them to colonize your heart, as Buddhist teacher Jack Kornfield says.

But wait, there's more: Definitely keep your journey to calmness underway, because you will need to come from an exceptionally centered place to be on both sides of the next skill: transparency in dealing with others. This will make you stronger, I promise! Read on….

CHAPTER 6

TRANSPARENCY PREVENTS DYSFUNCTION

"All streams flow to the sea
because it is lower than they are.
Humility gives it its power."
—*Lao Tzu*

Reflecting on the above quote, I encourage you to think of transparency as a form of humility—and therefore as an approach that will give you tremendous power as a leader. This is the other chapter that I almost started the book with, because I find transparency to be one of the most essential attributes of a healthy and thriving workplace.

In a workplace where transparency is absent, dysfunction results. My observation of many dysfunctional settings is not limited to the entertainment industry, because I had a wide and humbling variety of day jobs before becoming a TV writer. I was a short-order cook in a bar, and I drove the golf-cart tours at the Warner Bros. studio lot, just to name a couple. What I've seen is that, across all walks of life, a lack of transparency and clarity can cause toxicity.

I've seen clarity withheld out of indecision, out of a desire to control others, and out of a resistance to committing to timelines and metrics. All of those motivations come from fear—fear of making the wrong call, fear of not being able to hoard all the answers and wield them like currency, and fear of falling short of expectations.

But the great news is that providing clarity, and being transparent, will get you what you actually want: better accomplishments from your team in support of your shared goal.

Here's an example of how transparency prevents dysfunction. When I lead a writers' room, every Sunday at 1 p.m. I send an email to the entire team to set the schedule for the week. I tell them what my specific goals and time-sensitive commitments are for each upcoming day, so they can plan their lives accordingly (for example—"I'll be in a sound mix on Tuesday at 2 p.m., so instead of an afternoon session that day we'll have independent study for people to work on their scenes, which means that's a great afternoon for your life errands this week."). I find that it's incredibly valuable for people to know when to concentrate their energy and just as valuable to avoid draining a team's energy, which is what happens when you make them needlessly stick around and spin their wheels.

You can provide respectful clarity on a macro level as well. On *Nancy Drew*, I instituted a practice of regular "fireside chats" (this is actually what they were called on the production team's schedule) where I would Zoom with all the department heads and share a bird's-eye view of what was coming down the road. This forecasting for the coming months might include story plans that would require, for instance, a black-tie cocktail party with a hundred extras in attendance, a mystical relic dating back to the Civil War era, or a shorefront location looking out at the open sea. By giving the costumes, casting, props, art, locations, VFX, and camera departments an early heads-up about what to prepare for, I accomplished several enormously helpful things for my team:

- advance notice to research and acquire the most cost-efficient solutions,
- sufficient turnaround time to prepare a multitude of necessary physical components,
- creative inclusion to get folks excited about collaborating on key elements of our shared goals,
- empowerment to respond and innovate at the top of their game, instead of being forced to react and play catch-up; and
- preservation of energy and boosts for morale, due to all of the above.

The key is to provide an early heads-up and context for the big picture so that team members can improve their efforts with information and engagement about why the schedule is the way it is. And here's a bonus benefit of this practice: By holding yourself to a standard of setting and publicizing timelines, you will become more organized, which will increase and project your sense of calm (see chapter 5!).

I'm not suggesting that you broadcast goals that you might not reach during the upcoming week. I'm advising that you realistically game-plan for what you *can* do every seven days. If you're disappointed in what you think you can achieve in the coming week, that's an excellent diagnostic tool to understand what you need to rethink to get to your objectives and where to ask for help. *Declaring your intentions and making yourself transparent has a ripple effect of clarifying what* everyone *needs to do in order to accomplish your shared goals—which can only help you succeed.*

Getting clarity about your own upcoming schedule—and being radically honest with yourself about what's on your plate—can lead to the uncomfortable but critical realization that you may need more help and/or more time than originally anticipated. This does not make you a bad person (the window to my psyche is opening again). In my experience, asking for help and showing vulnerability in the moment will create the conditions where you can perform at a much higher level.

This can be as simple as requesting a reasonable extension on a deadline (I'm still learning this one as a longtime overachiever and recovering people pleaser, but it's an effective strategy when used judiciously and respectfully, and not nearly as disruptive as delivering something before it's ready).

Another effective strategy is to reschedule within a professional timeframe when conditions are temporarily preventing you from doing your best work. As veteran TV producer Lis Rowinski puts it, "It is not unkind to reschedule something if you're not going to show up prepared. Because if you show up unprepared, you're saying, 'Hey, I don't really value your time, but I'm going to take up a bunch of it,' and you're making things up on the spot, but it's not going to really advance the ball.

"I had a writer session on my calendar—we had four hours scheduled to work on a project—but it was the day after [I had a challenging issue to resolve with an employee], and I called the writer and said, 'I'm sorry, but I am not feeling creative, and we need to push [the meeting].' At first, he was bummed to reschedule, but when we did get back on the Zoom, I came prepared with a bunch of ideas, and we jumped right in. We got it all figured out and did it in a shorter amount of time. And that was because I'd rescheduled to a time when I could really be present and creative and there for the person, as opposed to keeping a meeting on the books when I knew I really didn't have it [together]."

Of course, it's not always easy for people to be this honest with each other. Folks want to save face, be polite, or act like they have it all together. But if you've worked among humans as I have, you've probably observed that everyone eventually always figures out what's really going on. So why waste time trying to hide reality?

In fact, why not smartly allocate time to a structured process where you openly acknowledge what's really going on for everyone, and use that information to improve the work environment and the work produced?

Great news: This process exists, and it's called a "360-degree peer review." Stay with me! It doesn't have to hurt. Let's see how they've successfully done this in a high-pressure, fast-paced, and mega-profitable field: the video game industry.

Case Study: The Video Game Industry and the 360-Degree Peer Review

Brad Marques has worked as the animation director for video game companies that produce some of the world's most popular games, including League of Legends. In his day, a standard and performance-boosting practice was the 360-degree peer review, where, a few times a year, every person in the department would take a week to simultaneously evaluate each other's performance. Peers would review each other laterally, supervisors would review their direct reports, and everyone else in the department would review their supervisor.

I can hear the gasps on the other side of this page. I'll say it again: Every department head received honest and extensive feedback about *their* performance as evaluated by the people they were supervising. People had the option to remain anonymous, but everyone was strongly encouraged to put their name on every evaluation, and the company was extremely watchful for any signs of retaliation following the review process. As in, if they found anyone retaliating against a colleague as a result of an unfavorable review, there would be severe consequences from the company.

Putting names on the evaluations did create stress, because it's uncomfortable and challenging to give and receive open critiques. But the review process also created a lot of trust, because the company fostered an environment where people were literally instructed to be as honest as possible, without fear of retaliation. That feedback was the start of a long broad conversation so that both sides leveled up. The end result of all this candid evaluation, and ongoing follow-ups to the evaluations, was that the company was fostering growth across the board.

In the peer reviews, they wrote about strengths and weaknesses and areas to work on. Then there was an open writing section—"Normal, good human stuff, non-corporate-y stuff," Marques said. "If you didn't have a lot of feedback for a particular colleague, your own feedback for yourself was, maybe I should find a way to work with that person more. It was really cool." And the feedback could be blunt and extensive, but that was a valuable aspect of the process.

"If everyone is willing to give it and take it with honesty and openness, and trust that it's not going to be weaponized or given or received with ill intent, the whole team rises together for the benefit of the product. But it doesn't work if even one person holds back or doesn't want to receive feedback in that way. I got my whole team to get after those peer reviews, even folks from Korea who had come up in a culture that usually did not allow people to critique their superiors," Marques added.

From the get-go, he said, you have to set the expectation that the peer review is happening on a preannounced schedule so that everyone gives feedback at the same time. If you know on day one that this 360-degree peer review is coming every few months with the goal of the whole team rising together, then the dynamic of every interaction changes, including how leaders treat their team members. Knowing that you're going to have all of your team remembering the moment that you responded to an idea you didn't like, you'll choose to behave more respectfully, because you know you'll be accountable for how you treat the team.

He pointed out that every industry would benefit from these kinds of peer reviews, maybe none more so than the ones that proclaim themselves to be all about individual voices. "In creative fields, we're so bold and independent, and we say all kinds of things on social media, but no one has the courage to intentionally solicit candid feedback from the full teams we lead," Marques said. "It's hilarious."

$$\oplus$$

In the same spirit as a 360-degree review, there's a practice in writers' rooms called "the roundtable." Not everyone likes the egalitarianism of this method, but I stand by it. On the shows

I run, when a writer has completed a draft, they send it to the entire writing staff to read, and then the entire writing staff assembles around the meeting table (or on Zoom) to give feedback. Even though I'm leading the staff, my scripts go through the exact same process as the scripts of the first-year writers. I'm always so glad I solicit the critiques of my colleagues, because the end result always improves when the brainpower of multiple professionals is applied in a collegial and constructive way. Another great benefit of this method is that everyone on the staff gets to see the real-time refinement of each other's work. It demystifies and teaches at the same time. And, very importantly, it's an opportunity for everyone to see what works for my subjective taste and objective metrics, and what doesn't.

In short, the roundtables in my writers' rooms provide an ongoing system for sharing transparency about what I want. Your workplace might not have an exact parallel to scripts that can get feedback from writing staffs, but I bet with just a little intentionality you can find a way for your team to actively share transparency in all directions.

I like the roundtable process because in its absence people get subjected to a sort of "mystery box" approach. Everyone's work gets sent into the mystery box of their boss's office, and something else comes out the other end, with very little understanding imparted about why the boss made changes along the way. This is frustrating and disempowering and also teaches people nothing.

Another thing that happens with the mystery box approach is that, without clear communication, people can be left feeling that their leader is acting unpredictably because the leader doesn't know what they want. I would say that many leaders do know what they want, but they're too afraid/polite/conflict-avoidant/

impatient to actually say it out loud in a specific and understandable way.

Well, get ready to say it out loud. I promise you'll be glad you did.

⊕

If you just had a knee-jerk reaction of "it takes way too long to explain what I want to my subordinates. When they don't deliver what I want, I'm just going to step in and fix it myself. And then I'll save them the discomfort of showing them what they did wrong," then you are missing the huge *time-saving rewards* of transparency.

I'll use an example from the business environment of TV writing, because I believe the lessons of this are applicable to many different work situations. Also, it might prompt empathetic dismay and/or amusement to get a glimpse of the behind-the-scenes journey that sometimes happens before your favorite TV show reaches a screen near you.

Almost every TV writer has had a version of this experience at some point their career: They spend weeks coming up with the ideas for a TV episode, laboriously work those ideas out in great detail with continuous input from others on the writing staff and executives at the studio and network, and then spend more weeks writing and refining a fifty-page script that they've poured their heart and soul into. They email this script to their boss the showrunner. Then a few days later, the showrunner sends a revised draft of that script to the studio/network—except many of the writer's words, ideas, dialogue exchanges, action set pieces, character moments, you name it, have vanished entirely, to be replaced by the showrunner's words and ideas. Sometimes *all* of the writer's words have vanished (this is called a "page-one rewrite" and happens more frequently than you might imagine), though usually their name is still on the title page under "Written By."

I don't provide this anecdote to demonize showrunners. I have revised and rewritten scripts myself, always with practical reasons—maybe we ran out of time to give the writer another crack at it, maybe we were working with a writer who couldn't mimic the style of the show or the voices of the characters, or maybe we had a production change (such as having to create an entirely new role because an actor was no longer available to continue on the show) that necessitated a fast and complicated reworking of storylines across multiple episodes. And part of being a showrunner is that you almost always do a final revision pass on every script before it goes up the chain.

However! In many instances, writers see a script (at the same time that the rest of their colleagues see it) that has been significantly changed from what they turned in *without any explanation at all* for why their words were erased. Like, no reasons, no discussion, no opportunity to talk through the issues together. Crickets. This is, to say the least, disheartening to the person whose work got unraveled and redone. But to the leader, it's a symptom of a vicious cycle where the leader is not training their team members to *hit the mark themselves*. Instead, over and over, we see this series of events:

> Step 1. The team member does what they can with limited information about how to satisfy the leader.

Step 2. The leader receives the work and is unsatisfied with it.

Step 3. The leader does the same work again, by themselves, as if step 1 never happened at all.

In the above vicious cycle, both sides get more and more frustrated and tired and may eventually grow resentful of each other. All of this reduces the efficiency of the work as well as the enjoyment of it, and those constraints will negatively impact the quality of the work itself. The good news is that intervention is possible. (Hint: It's within step 1.) The challenging news is that intervening requires an investment of time and transparency. You'll have to slow down your pace in order to be honest and *present* with your team—and I realize those items are in escalating order of difficulty—but the payoff for future you is so very worth it.

Here's what I mean by intervening. If your team member has completed a task that's not to your satisfaction, then you need to specifically and neutrally tell them how they need to do it next time. You're giving them the information they need to meet your standards, and you're giving yourself the gift of not dreading the results the next time you assign them a task.

Being neutral hopefully isn't too much of a challenge for you, but if it is, I recommend doing the following things before a conversation about work products: Hydrate yourself, have something to eat so that you're not speaking from a hangry place (I have made this mistake myself in the past), and keep the conversation on the task and not the person who did the task.

Being specific can be its own challenge, but I promise that no one you work with is an actual psychic. Very often, even when we think we're being perfectly clear, what we say leaves room for interpretation, confusion, and incorrect guesswork—unless and until we spell it out for those around us. Time and time again, I have learned the following the hard way:

> **_Team members do better work_**
> **_when you are relentlessly_**
> **_clear about what you want._**

Relentless doesn't mean rude or aggressive. It just means that you leave no room for doubt. Encourage people to ask questions, request that people explain the task back to you in their own words, and get their agreement on what the instructions and standards are. In other words, don't just tell your team member what you don't want; tell them exactly what you *do* want. This method has a much higher likelihood of producing excellent results than vaguely asking someone to do better and then hoping it all turns out okay.

For example, when I Zoomed with a junior writer on *Nancy Drew* to walk her through why I was making changes to her script, I took time to give multiple examples of the characters' dialogue and how the same sentiment and information sounds entirely different when expressed by the various characters on the show after factoring in each individual's speech pattern, demeanor, and fictional background. This "voice pass" is something that showrunners often do on someone else's script, but it uses up time that could be better spent on (a) executive-level decisions that only the showrunner can make and (b) by the individual writer in improving their skills so they can start to regularly deliver drafts that meet the desired standard.

The above strategy can be summed up in wisdom I learned from TV director Andi Behring:

Slow down
to speed up.

Applied globally, this motto is something you can remind yourself of when you're tempted to rush through a task, because doing it more carefully the first time will greatly reduce the risk of making mistakes along the way, and the end result is that you don't waste additional time going back and correcting those mistakes. Right now, though, I'm applying the motto to being respectfully present for a team member while you have a clear and specific conversation about what you want. That conversation isn't over until your team member articulates a full understanding of what you have just told them.

This may take some time (during which you'll slow down), but in the end, you will get the results you want *so much faster* from your fully informed team members, without the aggravation, inefficiency, and demoralization of having the work redone multiple times, either by them or by you. At that point, you get to speed up, and you'll be able to maintain that increased speed in a sustainable way because you've been transparent with your team.

Let's say for the sake of argument that you'll set aside two hours to sit with a team member and explain to them—in a specific, neutral, and respectful way—exactly what you need from them when they complete a task for you. And you'll use part of that time to have them summarize their new understanding of what you want. As in, politely ask them to literally say it out loud back to you, which might feel a bit awkward at first, but it's far less awkward and way less time-consuming than receiving unsatisfactory work over and over again and having to fix it yourself, over and over again. The intervention is not complete until both of you are on the same page with an agreed-upon set of expectations and standards for the work requested.

"Two hours?" you might exclaim. "I don't have that kind of time in a day. I eat meals at my desk. I don't see my kids. I can't remember the last time I went to the gym. I'm already behind on my own work, and *my* work is what keeps the earth rotating on its axis. Why should this underperforming team member get two hours of my precious and nonexistent time? How does that math make sense?"

But it does make sense, because let's do the other math. If it takes you two hours to redo your team member's work the next time they fail to meet your (currently murky) standards, then future you is already sacrificing that much time anyway. If your team member messes up a second time because you couldn't be bothered to be clear with them before, then you're looking at a loss of four hours down the line. And so on.

Whereas, for an up-front investment of two hours and the manageable and worthwhile discomfort of radical clarity, you have now freed up *all those hours* that future you would have otherwise spent gnashing your teeth and complaining about your team member while you redid their task for them, again.

If you don't have time to sit with a colleague for two hours, then break it up into smaller chunks, like one-hour sessions on two different days or thirty minutes a week for four weeks if the workflow can accommodate that. Or, make room for a few fifteen-minute sessions during the course of a couple of weeks, and discipline yourself to convey your information and training within that time. If you can't find fifteen minutes a week for an important improvement to the efficiency of your overall workflow, then I recommend you reconsider how your days are unfolding. The prime culprit for time drains: Over the course of any given week, are there really not fifteen minutes that you can divert from looking at social media on your phone? (I'm speaking to myself as well, by the way.)

However, maybe the issue is not just that you don't feel like allocating the time. Maybe the issue is that you think you're sparing your colleagues' feelings by not showing them what they did wrong. Or possibly you are deeply conflict avoidant and as a result you're needlessly living in fear. Be comforted! One of the key takeaways of this entire book is that *when you are (courteously) clear with a subordinate about how they missed the mark, you are doing them a giant favor.* Because if you don't tell them how they missed the mark, you are setting them up to miss the mark again next time, and then you'll experience the same tension of finding ways to avoid the discomfort of speaking about the issue directly.

And guess who suffers for that? You do, because you have created and reinforced a system where you are unclear about what you need, you get stressed out because you don't feel you can be honest with people who haven't met your standards, and then you shoulder the burden of being the lone savior who has to fix it by yourself every time.

Becoming the lone savior might not have been your conscious intention but take a minute to think about what you might be getting out of it emotionally, such as: When you're the only one who knows how to fix things, does it make you feel needed, and therefore a little more secure in your own job? Or is it that it makes you feel in control, and therefore a little more important and/or less afraid of upsetting yourself or others?

I'm not saying these things to judge you. It's understandable to want to feel all of these things. I trust that you are needed and important regardless, and I empathize with not wanting to experience upset feelings or cause them in others. But if you're not transparent with people, you are actually setting in motion a cycle that will end up making your team less productive—which will leave some of your potential success on the table, and we're here to get you all the success you can possibly get.

If you are trapped either consciously or unwittingly in this kind of cycle, there's good news: You can break this cycle and find increased success by practicing several doable skills. First up is *the skill of saying no.*

How to Tell People No While Remaining Neutral and Professional: Concrete Tips

People sometimes hate to say no, especially in the entertainment industry. As the saying goes (attributed to film critic Pauline Kael), Hollywood is the only place where you can die of encouragement. I take this to mean that by not definitively saying no, you're giving people breadcrumbs of illusory hope while the thing they're waiting for slowly withers on the vine—often as you fully expected it would. In these cases especially, *saying no is a form of kindness.*

A handy comparison chart:

The thing that's making you hesitate	The benefit to them	How to say no
Their feelings will be hurt.	Don't string them along. Eventually they will figure it out, and at least this way you give them the dignity of being treated like an adult whose world doesn't revolve around you.	Be respectful/clear.
They're going to be mad.	They can move on.	Be gentle/clear.
They'll be disappointed/out of chances.	They can move on.	Be kind/clear.
They'll think I'm being unfair.	They'll find out what is actually keeping them from getting a yes.	Be specific/constructive.
They'll throw a fit/make a fuss/punish me emotionally.	They'll get practice in handling disappointment professionally when you maintain your boundaries.	Be calm/clear.

That last one is especially hard for people pleasers and recovering people pleasers, so I can relate if you struggle with this. But gradually, you'll build the muscle for being okay when other people are upset, and you will start to get pieces of your own life back. (The window to my psyche is, again, opening.)

And because I so empathize with how difficult it can be to tell people no, especially if you haven't practiced it a lot, let me break it down for you even further.

It helps to (courteously and professionally) start the conversation by setting expectations so the other person doesn't spend part of the conversation mistakenly thinking that it's going to go in their favor. It's also so that you don't get accidentally prevented from saying no because you get so caught up in conversational niceties and beating around the bush that you have to end the conversation because you run out of time.

Here are some examples of how it could go:

- First, set expectations: This isn't the phone call I wanted to make, but… / This will be tough to hear, but… / I've made a decision that will be disappointing to you, but…
- Then rip off the Band-Aid: After a lot of thought, I'm not renewing your contract. / It has come to my attention that your behavior doesn't meet my minimum standards of professionalism. / I'm going to respectfully decline pursuing this project with you.
- Finally, give brief and honest context for the no in a cordial way, and provide next steps if needed, but keep it short and sweet. Once people clearly hear no from you, they will often be fine with exiting the conversation sooner than later anyway.

When you need to tell someone no, if you're experiencing anxiety about it, it might help to write your remarks out and practice the conversation. You can practice with a trusted friend, but out loud to yourself will do the trick, and it won't risk having delicate information spilled to others. (I'm sure your friends are very trustworthy, but everyone is human and as the saying goes: If you want to keep something a secret, tell no one; if you want everyone to know something, tell it to one person and tell them it's a secret.)

After delivering your no, be silent for a short time, to let the other person feel their feelings, gather their thoughts, ask questions, and respond to you. During any conversation that ensues, stay on message. The message being that you're having an empathetic conversation because you've made a decision to say no to something, for a few specific reasons. Repeat the "rip off the Band-Aid" stage if the other person is resisting acceptance of your decision.

The word *decision* is key. This conversation is simply about relaying a decision that you've already made. You're just reporting the facts. Stick to your decision and your talking points. And after you've given the other person a few minutes to absorb your no and respond if they need to, then end the conversation as quickly as is gracefully and professionally possible.

How to Have Other Transparent Conversations Outside Your Comfort Zone: Concrete Tips

Here are two more areas where you might sometimes retreat into a comfort zone of staying silent/avoiding specifics/making nice with white lies:

- when the truth is that you don't like something, and
- when the truth is that you don't have the answer to a question or situation.

It's okay to feel discomfort about these things, and it's okay to wish you had all the answers all the time; you're human. What is not okay from a business perspective is when you hide from uncomfortable communication simply because you don't like being uncomfortable. If you want to be an effective leader who becomes as successful as possible, then you need to center yourself and learn to tolerate discomfort.

"But I'm successful, and I stay in my comfort zone all the time," you might protest. "People have learned to work around my comfort zone, and I still get results. Yes, maybe people might like some more candor from me, but why is that necessary when I can protect their feelings and maintain my power in the situation by withholding information (possibly not in that order of importance to my comfort zone)?"

With the caveat that all of this communication still needs to be professional and respectful, here's why candor is necessary and fruitful:

> **Transparency will liberate your
> team to please you better.**

And it will free up their energy to work harder for you (this being the energy that was previously burned away by trying to read your mind, quietly swallowing resentment at your cagey silences, or harboring mistrust of your insincere pleasantries). But transparency is not just a matter of freeing up energy. Transparency's targeted benefit is that people will care more about the work they do for you because they know you're being honest with them. It's true that they might experience some of their own discomfort along the way. But occasional discomfort is (a) part of being a grown-up with a job and (b) a worthwhile trade-off for specific information about how to do that job better than before.

If honesty sounds scary and disempowering to you, consider this situation: Have you ever given a friend a gift (let's say a nice green shirt) and heard them say how much they loved it, only to never ever see them wear it, not even once? Makes you second-guess yourself the next time you're supposed to buy them a gift, right? And it makes you less inclined to go all-out on the next gift, doesn't it? I'm not saying it would feel awesome to hear them say that they didn't like your gift at all. But they could sincerely thank you for your thoughtful gift, and then they could candidly say that they might not wear the shirt very often because they don't think green looks good on them. They could also transparently add that they're going to keep the shirt in a place of honor because seeing it will be a happy reminder of you and your cherished friendship.

Having heard all that, you could candidly ask them what color they *do* like in shirts. If the answer is, say, purple, then I bet you'd be willing to look for a purple shirt in a positive frame of mind, because you would trust that you now had a specific understanding of how to get the best payoff for your time and energy invested.

So, here are doable, neutral, professional ways to say "I don't like it" and "I don't have the answer." Friendly encouragement: People will not respect you less for being clear with them (as long as you're not abrasive or dismissive when you're providing clarity). Also, these aren't the only options out there; these are just starting points.

⊕

Ways You Can Say "I Don't Like It" While Remaining Professional and Neutral

First, express appreciation and acknowledgment that work has been done, especially if it's work that you requested! Examples: "Thank you for sending in this report…" "I appreciate the work that went into this…" "I know this new role on the team is important to you."

Next, rip off the Band-Aid and keep your statement as neutral as possible by making your assessment about the work rather than about the person who did the work, unless your critique is literally about someone's behavior. (Notice that there is no "but" that precedes these statements. Your gratitude in part 1 of this stands completely separate from and unaffected by the fact that a critique is next.)

Examples: "From my reading of it, the report doesn't fully answer the question that prompted this task…." "We need to pivot in a different direction in order to stay on budget…." "It has come to my attention from multiple sources that your behavior towards your colleagues does not meet my minimum standards for professionalism."

Finally, present your request for next steps: "Please revise the report by the end of the week to provide specifics on *XYZ* metrics, in answer to the question we're researching…." "The budget is capped at *X* dollars for this project, so I need you to rethink this plan to fit inside that constraint; please send me the new plan by Monday at one p.m….." "I've scheduled a meeting with HR at three p.m. tomorrow to discuss our pathway forward."

And then give the other person a reasonable and finite amount of time to respond/ask for additional clarification. The finite time (for example, another ten minutes in the conversation or a follow-up email the next business day) doesn't mean that you can't revisit or continue a conversation if you can't reach consensus and understanding right away. But it will help you not derail your entire day around this conversation, and it will give everyone time to decompress from the experience of relaying and hearing, "I don't like it." (I never said that these tactics wouldn't require energy and fortitude, and it's important to refill your emotional and psychological well after these conversations.)

Getting people to commit to the completion of next steps and getting them to deliver on those commitments is central to chapter 8 on accountability, but you'll notice a hint of those tools in how specific the above requests and their accompanying timelines and context are.

Ways You Can Say "I Don't Have the Answer" While Remaining Professional and Neutral

First, acknowledge that a question has been asked, that an issue has been raised, or that a decision is needed. (This goes back to the importance of replying to an email with "Received." When you don't even indicate that you are aware of unanswered questions that are causing a bottleneck in your team's workflow, you look at best out of touch and at worst passive aggressive. Neither one of those will produce the morale, dedication, and collaboration that will lead to success.) Examples: "I understand your question...." "That's a valid issue...." "I'm aware that I need to make a decision on this before the group can move forward."

Next, openly acknowledge that you don't yet have the answer, the timeline, or control concerning the issue on the table. Examples: "I don't have the answer yet...." "Our funding request is pending a decision, but first we'll need to find out what happens with other budget cuts in the company...." "I am still debating what serves our vision best."

Finally, set a timeline for when you *will* have the answer. (More about this powerful business muscle in chapter 8 on accountability.) For example: "I'll send an email by ten a.m. on Friday to tell you when I'll have my answer." This example actually applies to all three of these hypothetical conversations. You're not promising an answer on Friday at 10 a.m. You're promising that on Friday at 10 a.m. you'll tell the team *when* you'll have an answer.

If you can't control the timeline of when an answer will emerge, then own up to that too. For example: "I unfortunately have no way of knowing when corporate headquarters will make its decision on budget cuts. Given this reality, let's meet at ten a.m. tomorrow for thirty minutes to discuss what choices we have going forward."

It may be humbling or even secretly scary to contemplate being transparent with your team in the ways I'm proposing. But I assure you it's okay to admit it when you're confronted with daunting circumstances beyond your control.

In fact, when you disclose those circumstances (with equanimity of course), people simply see that you're not oblivious or delusional, which actually builds their confidence in you because you've demonstrated your grasp on reality. (If you're like me, at some point in your journey you've been in a workplace where the leader fully denied or ignored a reality that everyone else was painfully aware of. So you know the kinds of quiet eye-rolling and loss of morale that result from watching your supervisor stubbornly move forward with blinders on.)

Not that this gets you off the hook for looking for ways to address whatever circumstances are challenging your team. But people will respect you more if you don't ignore the elephant(s) in the room. When they have full context for the constraints you're facing, they'll know you're treating them as adult professionals, and they will be more inclined to participate as such.

In other words, if you infantilize your team by not looping them into the realities you're dealing with, you're setting them (and therefore yourself) up for failure, and that's the opposite of what we're after here.

So, quick regroup on transparency strategies, and all of this needs to be cordial and professional in execution:

1. Give your team advance info on schedules so they can plan their lives.
2. Share big-picture plans with your team as a means to empower them.
3. Tell people no, instead of stringing them along.
4. Tell people you don't like something, instead of letting them spin their wheels.
5. Tell people you don't have the answer, instead of leaving them hanging.
6. Tell your team what you *do* want, instead of expecting them to read your mind.

7. Take the time to teach your team how to hit the mark for you, instead of making them fail over and over because you've given them insufficient information.

And now that you and your team are completely on the same page, we'll come to perhaps the toughest advice of all:

Ask for help.

You might immediately think, "I can't possibly ask for help. I'm a person who is a strong authority figure/a woman/a person of color/LGBTQ+/over fifty/a man/differently abled/young/new to the job/very established in my field/insert another identifier here—and therefore I can never show that I'm human or else people won't take me seriously anymore and then my authority will be undermined." But is your authority being shored up by burning yourself out and resenting your team for not knowing how to help you?

Asking for help does entail some vulnerability. But vulnerability—when acknowledged constructively and maturely—is not weakness. It's not weakness to know your own mortal limitations. It's not weakness to ask for help when you are marshaling the strengths of those around you while freeing yourself, the leader, for the high-level decisions and guiding vision. And in the meantime, you are fostering your team members' awareness of how integral each of them is to your common goal—because you're respectfully acknowledging that none of you can get there alone. Vulnerability and transparency will build you a bridge to community, and that community will generate the conditions for success.

⊕

Executive Highlights: Transparency

This section is for the people who avoided reading this chapter because they'd rather keep things to themselves as a way to feel safe and empowered. Here's a quick rundown of how acting with transparency will actually bring those people greater peace of mind and further their careers.

Snack-sized takeaway: Transparency does not diminish you or decrease your leverage in work interactions. Transparency is a sign of self-assurance, because you're demonstrating that you have the confidence to be honest and open. Transparency is a bridge to effective collaboration.

Business benefit: When you provide an honest, realistic, and timely assessment of a situation, along with a meaningful window into your process, your team will be much better equipped to strategize how to help you achieve your shared goals. Transparency also improves morale by treating people like the adults they've been hired to be. Better morale equals better results.

Sustainable strategy: Every week, give the team a brief but clear heads-up about your shared goals, in a way that forecasts the shape, schedule, and intentions of the next five business days. You will be amazed at the exponential goodwill and productivity generated by your regular road maps, because you'll consistently show the team that you respect their time.

Seriously, try this at home: When you don't know the answer to a question, immediately say these words: "I don't have that answer yet." The "yet" is important. Because the next thing you add is this: "But by [stated time], I will let you know when you can expect my answer." This relieves pressure in all directions (you're not promising an answer at that stated time—you're promising when you'll provide a timeline for your answer). And, crucially, this way you do not leave others hanging in a demoralizing, infuriating, and unprofessional void of uncertainty and silence.

Even if you're not the boss yet: Ask neutral questions to prompt clarity from those around you—clarity about expectations, deliverables, timelines, and contexts. Ask questions and dial in specifics until you've articulated mutual agreements about *who will do what by when, and why* (Birgit Zacher Hanson's strategy for success—see chapter 8 on accountability). If people resist giving you specifics because they're transparency-avoidant, gently remind them of your shared goals (desired, big-picture outcomes) and request that they provide you with the tools (specifics) to get them what they want.

To lead with transparency, you'll have to expand your tolerance for the discomfort of *frustrating other people from time to time.* No one likes to hear "no," and they don't tend to be fans of "I don't like your idea" either. However, conveyed respectfully, both of those statements will save you and your team labor, energy, and morale while you make your vision clear.

But wait, there's more: So far, we've got inclusion, kindness, trust, love, calm, and transparency—all great tools to bring our team's whole selves to whatever process we're engaged in. However, if we're going to bring our whole selves, then we need to look at ways to weave in our commitments, passions, and priorities outside of the workplace. "Balance" might be elusive because that word implies a perfect equilibrium, and lasting equilibrium among conflicting and overlapping forces is frequently not attainable for those of us who live in the real world. However, *navigation* and *integration* are possible, and to find out how to set yourself up for success when integrating your work life and your personal life, read on....

CHAPTER 7

WORK-LIFE INTEGRATION ELEVATES RESULTS

"Don't hit your head on the glass ceiling on the way out."

That's what an executive producer said (in front of the assembled writers' room) to a high-ranking writer who was also a single mother when she left at 5:30 p.m. to pick up her toddler from childcare one day. We were working on a TV show that had a particularly toxic ecosystem with constant staff turnover, rock-bottom morale, and a nonstop workflow scramble that caused massive budget overages and hampered creativity because of the cultural dysfunction.

The above quote is just one example of the snide and dismissive comments I heard for years when I was coming up the ranks of TV writers' rooms. In the entertainment industry, and in many others as well, there's an attitude (often explicitly stated, and ever-present regardless) that work comes first, no matter what, and that to attend to your personal life in any way is a grave character flaw and an indication that you lack commitment to the job.

A devil's advocate argument about this situation would say, "But look at *XYZ* television show. Yes, the showrunner was unbelievably toxic and abusive and later got sued for documented harassment with a multi-million-dollar settlement awarded to the plaintiff, but the series was critically acclaimed, and the ratings were very successful. So one, it was worth the toxic behavior, and two, maybe the toxic behavior was even necessary to get that artistic and financial result."

I strongly disagree with the assessment that toxic behavior is ever *worthwhile* or *necessary*, regardless of its products. My response to the devil's advocate is this: First, if the studios and networks footing the bill for these TV shows made their funding and contracts strictly conditional on humane behavior, then leaders would find a way to meet those conditions to continue receiving the financial and creative privilege of making art. In other words, if the consequence for inhumane behavior was that all the money would be dried up, then the dynamics would self-correct accordingly.

Second, how much *better* could the result be in any field if a huge amount of time, energy, and money weren't squandered on enabling domineering egos and dysfunctional processes? The only way to find out is if we change our culture one workplace at a time—which is my goal in writing this book.

Toxic behavior in the workplace is a very broad topic, so I'm going to focus this chapter on just one kind of toxic behavior—namely, an abusive leadership style that demands nonstop labor at the expense of a personal life. Nonstop labor meaning: long hours in the office or at the work site, work emails and calls and text messages 24/7, rigid schedules, a culture that frowns on taking any kind of time off, and even subtle punishments for anything that doesn't completely subject your time to the whims of the boss. It's all too common for short-sighted leadership to severely impair the ability of team members to have a life outside of work. This causes frustration, burnout, and related struggles—all of which eat away at productivity and performance. Witnessing this lack of balance early in my career, I began to question: Isn't there a smarter way to manage people and resources?

I discovered a very clear answer by watching the goats at the Atlanta zoo.

Case Study: The Goats at the Atlanta Zoo

There are two paddocks in the goat area: a petting zoo where screaming kids run around and swat at placidly unfazed goats with grooming brushes and an adjacent area that the goats can step away to when they need a break, no questions asked. When the goats feel like returning to the madness, they walk themselves back in through the swinging gate to the kids' area. As the goat manager explained to me, "Every goat in the petting zoo *wants* to be here *and knows it can leave anytime.*"

This is the core of how I run a writers' room. I encourage people to go to dentist appointments, school plays, destination weddings, you name it. Everyone in my writers' rooms knows they can leave anytime—and because I give them agency over their own schedules, they actually want to be there more. When you offer people the flexibility to live their lives—when you embrace and model stepping away for the sake of health, rest, and relationships—people actually contribute more efficiently, more energetically, and with an appreciation that leads to longevity in the job. Once again, the humane approach nets you exponential rewards.

And I'll pull from this a daring assertion: *Morale equals money.*

Morale is difficult to quantify, but if you're reading this book, it's likely that you've experienced a work environment with low morale at some point in your life, and you'd love to know how to avoid it in the future (or fix it in the present, if you're in that unfortunate circumstance right now). Hopefully you've also experienced a work environment with good morale at some point in your professional life for comparison. Either way, here are some causes and effects for low morale, with the resulting impact on productivity. (These may seem intuitive because they're so widespread, but it's surprising to me how rarely people articulate them.)

Cause	Effect	Impact on outcomes
Long hours	Fatigue	Work results suffer
Inefficient use of time	Slowdown in productivity	Work results suffer
Lack of boundaries around work	Resentment	Work results suffer
Not enough time to take care of basic personal needs like doctors' appointments and childcare pickups/relief	Stress/distraction/outside challenges	Work results suffer

Attitude that attending to your personal life shows weakness and lack of commitment to work	Emotional toll	Work results suffer

The flip side of all this is that if you intentionally cultivate and encourage work-life integration for your team, you will get better business results. The opposite model:

Cause	Effect	Impact on outcomes
Reasonable hours	Better-rested team	Work results improve
Efficient use of time	Optimized productivity	Work results improve
Clear boundaries around work	Healthy professionalism	Work results improve
Enough time to take care of basic personal needs like doctors' appointments and childcare pickups/relief	Focused calm	Work results improve
Attitude that attending to your personal life is a crucial way to foster career longevity through preventing burnout	Stronger mental health and increased attachment to the humane business setting	Work results improve

Let's get even more intangible but even more crucial about morale. If you really want to foster morale, you need to create a work environment where people know that what matters to them on a personal level is *100 percent aligned with their day-to-day efforts.*

When I say, "what matters on a personal level," I'm not talking about hobbies, sports teams, or favorite foods, though all of those are fine things that can find a comfortable and enjoyable place in workday conversations and break rooms. I'm talking about core principles and the various ways in which people define themselves, their purpose on the planet, and their connection to what's around them—be it other individuals, larger communities, or guiding ideals. (Stay with me, Overworked Businessperson. I'll bring this back to your goal-oriented concerns in a minute.)

Read on for an example of what matters to me, and how it affected my commitments to two workplaces—once in a negative way and once in a positive way.

As a TV writer, producer, and creator, I am passionately against putting gun violence on screen. My intentionality around this emerged through my emotional response to the Sandy Hook tragedy in 2012. After that mass shooting in a grade school, I took a long look in the mirror and considered how the entertainment industry had played a role in the problem of gun violence in this country, through portraying gun violence on screen as empowering, exciting, sexy, commonplace, and above all *acceptable*.

With that in mind, I decided I didn't want to contribute to those normalizing and romanticizing characterizations on screen anymore, and resolved that, to whatever extent I had creative control over what I put on screen myself, I would make sure to keep guns out of my writing.

Having reached that clarity about what mattered to me, I still had to live in the real world—which included working for a boss whose views differed from mine. So here comes the negative example. A few years after Sandy Hook, I was on the staff of a TV show where my boss had written a scene containing—in my opinion—an unnecessary amount of gun violence. It was not just because it was a scene with multiple violent murders, but because there were other and (again in my opinion) more creative ways we could dispatch with those villains. So, I went into my boss's office and respectfully asked for a few minutes to voice my concerns about the gun violence in that scene and pitch a few alternative creative solutions to achieve the same outcome.

I'll give my former boss credit for hearing me out very courteously and for considering my objections—but the script didn't change, and the episode aired exactly as written. And when I saw that the storytelling on this particular show was antithetical to something that truly mattered to me as a human being, two things happened.

One is that I felt a little door close inside me. It's the little door that closes when you need to protect a true and valuable part of yourself because you've realized your current environment is antagonistic towards that true part of yourself. But I still needed the job, and I enjoyed and was learning from other aspects of it. So in order to keep doing my day-to-day work, my true self had to be partially denied and kept separate from my work self. I continued to work on that show for the remainder of the season, but I had to compartmentalize my own moral compass from what I was doing for a living. (It's no coincidence that I chose a compass graphic for both my book cover and my podcast logo.)

That said, here's the second thing that happened when I saw that what mattered to me didn't matter to my workplace: I decided that I needed to become a showrunner so that I could have the final word on not putting gun violence on screen. My determination led me in a straight line to become a showrunner after that, and in the shows that I run, my only creative rule is that there is no gun violence on screen.

In other words: When I saw that what mattered to me didn't matter to my workplace, that's when I started to actively plan my exit.

I'll say it even more bluntly for the Overworked Business people out there: If you disregard what matters to your team members, you will lose them. And then you will have to replace them. And both of those things will cost you money and make your life harder.

Conversely, paying attention to what matters to your team and manifesting that in your workplace environment reaps dividends and long-term benefits. So, here's the subsequent positive example: Some years later, I was offered a job in a pre-greenlight writers' room for an adaptation of a graphic novel that featured a tremendous amount of gun violence. I told the showrunner that my only hesitation in taking the job was the fact that I'm strongly against putting gun violence on screen.

The showrunner agreed with the points I raised, and as a result, he creatively adjusted the show so that the main characters specifically disavowed guns in the first episode and proceeded on their adventures without any firearms. I was extremely grateful that he was open to incorporating my viewpoint, and I took the job for a fraction of my normal salary rate. Not only that, but I felt so committed to the team's goals that I volunteered to share my script (and therefore half of its accompanying payment) with a younger writer so I could mentor them and make sure they received additional compensation for what we worked on together. The entire experience was a joy, and I contributed with extra enthusiasm and innovation because I knew my workplace valued me—not in spite of who I was, but because of who I was.

And all this because my new boss fostered an environment where my true self could come out and play at 100 percent. This is not to say that you have to reshape everything you're working on just to accommodate the personal values of one team member, though as you can see from the above example, if it improves the entire operation, then everybody wins. Regardless, when you respectfully solicit individuals' viewpoints and then try to avoid actions that are in direct opposition to what's important to your team members, you will have a more committed, engaged, and high-functioning workforce.

In contrast, when you make your team members compartmentalize their core identities and the things that matter to them most, you cut yourself off from their true, full potential. *When you force people to compartmentalize between their true self and their work self, you get a diminished version of that team member and a correspondingly diminished amount of their potential productivity.* (For you folks out there keeping score about productivity.)

Have you ever had to keep your mouth shut about something that really bothered you at work, because you needed to keep your head down, and you worried that speaking up or asking for a course correction would only make your life and your prospects worse? That kind of compartmentalization takes a toll on energy, focus, and caring about the goals of the team.

Because in our most essential, lizard-brain selves, if what matters to us is disregarded by those around us, then we withdraw a little (or a lot), as a survival mechanism. That survival mechanism is useful if our well-being is at risk (which, sadly, in some work environments it is). But retreating to that survival mechanism also burns energy. And you, like all humans, have a finite amount of energy to use in your various pursuits. If you're expending energy on a protective survival mechanism because your work environment doesn't align with and doesn't respect your internal compass, then you have that much less energy to devote to work.

When I think about team members' energy being left on the table, I always think about my teenage son Jackson running an eight hundred-meter race a couple of years ago. He won the race, his best friend came in a close second, and they did so pretty easily because of an overmatched field of competitors that day. So easily, in fact, that the race photo I have of the two of them shows them actually chatting and chuckling with each other as they make the final turn around the track. After the race, Jackson's coach came up to him and said with unsmiling tough love, "I don't want to see you talking during a race again. You're not there yet." Jackson shared this with me by way of saying that his coach did not have a sense of humor about that particular moment, but I was on the coach's side, and my comment to Jackson was: "Coach Rob isn't trying to settle for ninety-five percent of your best effort."

The same goes for you as a leader. Why are you trying to settle for 95 percent of your team's best effort (or 90 percent or 80 percent or much less than that in a toxic and demoralizing environment) when you can create a situation where they want to give 100 percent and actually do give 100 percent? In other words, you can be humane and nurturing and still go all-out to win—and you'll have a much better chance of doing so because you are creating conditions that support a healthy work-life integration. (In case you were wondering, being kind does not mean you have to stop wanting to win at things. I never said I wasn't competitive.)

> **When you foster and sustain an environment where people are encouraged and allowed to bring their full selves to the job, you get their full selves' worth of effort.**

A footnote to those of you who are eyeing the exits from your current situation because you can't be your full self: Sticking to your ideals is worth it on a business level. Now that I have the privilege of having more choices in the jobs I pursue, I've lost count of the number of times I've said no to taking on a project where gun violence was integral to the plot. But guess what? My productivity and my drive to succeed are even higher because my work self and my true self are 100 percent aligned.

I'm aware that not everyone has the luxuries of choice and agency that I do. Sometimes having to make accommodations between your private life, your work schedule, your personal views, and your business environment is just the nature of having a job in the world. Most people have had to do this at least once as adults. But this isn't a book about being resigned to and drained by past paradigms. This is a book about finding a better way forward.

I am here to advocate for this better way—its benefits and its possibilities—and to tell you that this alternate way is doable and attainable.

How so? I'm glad you asked. Here are two radical ideas to get you started.

$\oplus$

Two Radical Ideas to Create Alignment Between a Team Member's True Self and Their Work Self

Radical idea: Ask people what matters to them as human beings.

Ask with respect for people's boundaries and sensitivities, of course, and not all answers to these questions need to be shared with you or the group. The goal is to get team members thinking about what makes them tick and what their own version of their best self would be. Some questions in this direction: What experiences formed who you are? What realities and concerns are you sitting with in the present? What's most important to you right now and in the future? What are you proudest of in your life? What do you wish you had the opportunity to do, if you could be guaranteed of success in it? What message to the world would you shout from the mountaintops, if you knew for sure that people would listen and change as a result?

If you can set aside time during the workday for this, that's ideal, and when you have these conversations with genuine receptivity and warmth, they create valuable connection with and fascinating windows into those you work with. But a written form of these questions works too and might be a more comfortable format for any introverts on your team. (This kind of respectful space can help people feel that it's safe to reflect and share authentically.) The answers to these questions will serve as a personal manifesto for each team member.

By the way, you should be asking these questions of yourself and coming up with your own manifesto too. You're a member of the team, and as a leader you should equip yourself with full cognizance of what you're on this mortal plane to do. You'll get better outcomes in your work with this increased self-awareness and intentionality, and you'll also live a fuller and more satisfying life—not to put too fine a point on it.

Radical idea: In people's work lives, meaningfully incorporate what matters to them.

Once team members have their manifestos of purpose, message, and intention, encourage them to refer back to that manifesto as their North Star going forward. This goes for you as well. Everything in your life, every action that you take, every decision you make, every person you choose to spend your valuable time on Earth with will either take you closer to your North Star, or farther away from it. Everything else is lateral nonsense.

With this clarity at the front of your team members' minds, and with their manifestos articulated, you can jointly brainstorm ways for everyone to bring their work lives fully into alignment with their North Stars. This might be in a literal way, if there are aspects of your workplace that can support and develop team members' individual passions and interests. But it also might be in a way that healthily feeds the emotional aspects of the manifesto, the aspirations and passions that generate deep satisfaction and internal revitalization.

For example, if a team member delights in a hobby that is fueled by group engagement (Renaissance fair people, I'm looking at you) (also, I love the Ren fair), then you might look for ways to increase the sense of active community surrounding that team member in the workplace.

You do have to be prepared for the possibility that, after completing these explorations, some team members might conclude that their North Star is going to lead them away from their current work situation with you. Though this might be unsettling in the moment, I encourage you to see it as a positive development in the long run—certainly for them if they've realized that their purpose on the planet lies elsewhere but also for you if you come to a mutual and realistic assessment with this team member that they will at some point outgrow your workplace. That day was going to come anyway, and you're better off being looped in on their trajectory instead of receiving their two weeks' notice out of the blue at some future date.

So, quick regroup on tactics to foster work-life integration:

1. Delineate and respect boundaries around your team's personal lives and needs.
2. Ask your team members about what matters to them.
3. Incorporate those answers into the work they do.

The above will address work-life integration for each team member's individual situation. But how can you create a humane and sustainable culture for the entire workplace? To answer that question, I'm going to drill down on your number one priority: *time management.*

Time management encompasses a variety of ways for you to show respect to your team and to get the most out of them in return for your respect (that last part was for the Overworked Businesspeople who need to see value metrics). Fundamentally, I urge you to *loop people in on the planning schedule on a weekly and a daily basis.*

Next, and this may sound counterintuitive, but walk down the path with me on this—do your utmost to *limit the number of hours that people are at work,* because when you have a finite constraint on the hours you're meant to be working, you can incentivize people to be much more efficient with their time as a result. When there's no clear end to the workday or even to the length of a meeting, people learn to slow down their efforts, because what's the point of working more quickly, especially if they're working for the sort of boss who gives them side-eye if they leave before the clock strikes a certain minute?

Tell me you've never been in a situation where your boss wanted you to be sitting down at your desk for a predetermined span of hours, even though you had not been given enough work or direction to fill those hours or a timeline that gave a larger structure and context to what you were doing. Did you or did you not stretch out your work so that you looked busy when the boss came by, especially at the end of the day?

Finally, if you really want to supercharge your team's commitment to staying with you forever, *give people flexibility to plan their lives, even during work hours.* I realize that not every situation allows for a great deal of flexibility, but I fully believe that it's possible to be much more creative about scheduling than most people bother to be.

I am prepared for the knee-jerk reactions! Here are the three most common objections, with rebuttals gleaned from my successful experiences with time management and supporting commentary from Akima A. Brown, founder and executive director of Reel Families for Change, an organization that researches sustainable and empowering work-life solutions that enhance corporate performance and drive systemic change.

1. "Why should I let people go home early? I don't get to go home early."

Let me clarify that when I recommend limiting the hours that your team is at work, I'm not talking about the rest of your team galivanting off to the beach at 2 p.m. while you toil away in your office 'til midnight. Brown added to this: "There's a difference between 'going home early' and having a reasonable amount of hours worked in a day and having some flexibility to that. The belief is that more is more. But the longer you work, the higher probability of mistakes and accidents from human error. Harassment is more likely as well, because you have people whose emotional regulation is deteriorating, and their filters are unraveling. When people come into those spaces and experience those difficulties and those effects are not addressed, then they come back to work demoralized the next day, and the culture deteriorates even more.

"The question is, is there a reasonable schedule, a time-sensible day? Or are we going to *stay until I say we're leaving,* and now you have to keep driving people as you run them down, because you're not getting the desired outcomes when they're there. Or, you can get to the conclusion of your established and reasonable and expected block of time, *and people can trust that that's what the block of time is going to be*…and then you can get what you actually want during those hours. When people can't trust that the workday will end at an expected and agreed-upon time, they will stop trying hard, and the cycle will continue."

2. "Why should I give people time off or flexibility in their schedule? I had to come up this way."

I highly recommend that you stop punishing those around you for how you were treated in the past. I've found that *you can achieve much greater success by treating people humanely, no matter what your own previous experiences have been.*

If it gives you pleasure to control people's lives, I guarantee you that your team knows you are seeking that pleasure at their expense, and consequently they commit to you a little bit less, trust you a little bit less, and innovate for you a little bit less. All of those energy leaks are undermining their potential to help *you* succeed in *your* goals.

On the other hand, when you give people the respect of having agency in their own schedules, you show them that you value them as human beings, which makes them want to work harder for you. When you create a situation where rewards and approval come from task completion instead of hours logged, you incentivize your team to be more efficient and work faster, and they're more likely to perform successfully for you again and again. Crucially, offering flexibility in team members' schedules is a powerful incentive for them to stay with you instead of finding a different place to work.

Brown noted, "There's a belief that 'I need to see your face to know that you're working.' That's actually inefficient. Allow time flexibility, and if you have someone who's able to do more in less time and do it well, honor that." She cited parents as great examples of efficiency in the workplace: "Because parents know that their time is more limited and constricted, they tend to be more proficient in the use of their time, and they get more done in that time."

And speaking of parents, here's one of the most pernicious and inaccurate knee-jerk reactions that pervades many workplaces:

3. "If they were serious about this job, they wouldn't get pregnant/adopt a kid/have kids at all."

Brown had thoughts on this for sure. "That comes from the point of view of care as a personal problem, instead of a social issue. The nation recognizes that we need and want children, but having children is a problem when it inconveniences the system. We need a change in the system. It's a community matter; it affects us all. Can this individual have this child and raise that child and be a productive and supportive parent in their child's life? Women make up a huge part of the workforce, and if you want those people to be in your workforce, the system needs to expand to support them.

"The old perspective is that the person is broken [because of childcare needs or other perceived vulnerabilities] and has to be fixed like a problem. The bigger perspective is that the system is broken, and you lose so much when operational practices don't support everyone. So many people are excluded and can't participate. When we design a workplace structure and system that allows for what is possible for everyone, then everyone benefits from that."

If a more mercenary perspective helps you, look at it this way—having kids (and partners and aging parents and other people in our personal circles who we share responsibility for) creates an intense drive for job stability. When you create a work environment that supports the needs and schedules of parents and caregivers, then those parents and caregivers will do everything in their power to be worthy of staying in your employ, because your work environment sustains the complex and usually costly ecosystem of their intersecting obligations and priorities.

Using time management to enhance the work-life integration of your team members will result in higher productivity, increased commitment, and long-term loyalty. Now you just need a few basic tools to manage your time better. Get ready for three radical ideas. (And I realize that the first two ideas below are also mentioned in chapter 3 on trust, but I'm reinforcing them in this context because they're among the most important takeaways from this book.)

Three Radical Ideas to Foster Work-Life Integration Through Better Time Management

Radical idea: Start meetings on time.

How many situations have you been in where you knew that a meeting wouldn't start on time, so you didn't hurry to get there, and neither did anyone else, so the problem only got worse? How many meetings have you attended that began with many minutes of aimless small talk or stalling while waiting for stragglers to sign into the Zoom? If you start meetings on time and begin their substance immediately, people will figure it out and show up prepared to hit the ground running. Huge, related benefit: You establish a work culture where people's time is respected. If you respect other people's time, they will learn to respect yours.

Radical idea: End meetings on time.

This is one of the biggest momentum-killers I've seen during more than twenty years in highly paid professional environments—so big that I gave this problem its own paragraph. If people know from past experience that a meeting will simply drag on without a foreseeable conclusion, there's no incentive to move efficiently through items. If, however, you set an actual end time for the meeting—and stick to it—you will find yourself proceeding much more effectively, without digressions into rabbit holes of tangential discussions.

To avoid branching off into tangents, here's a pro tip from the world of TV production: When a subtopic comes up in a meeting, you ask for a sidebar meeting at a later time to discuss that subtopic, and you keep the flow of the stated meeting going. Huge related benefit: By keeping the meeting focused and by concluding it at the scheduled time, people can plan for what they do *after* the meeting, whether it's get to their next meeting, get back to the rest of their work, or head home for the day.

Another useful tactic: Even if the meeting starts late, still end it on time! And if you haven't finished what you needed to do, convene an additional meeting to complete those items. No one wants to have additional meetings, so this will incentivize people to start the next meeting on time because there has now been a *consequence* for not being organized enough or respectful enough to arrive and begin punctually.

Radical idea: Comp time.

Different people want different pockets of time off. Parents of young kids will love you forever if you suggest that they work a half day on Halloween (or even take the entire day off). If you have the ability to offer this without having to ask them to make up the missed hours at another time, then great. But if it's necessary (for team productivity or because of how compensation is structured) to have them swap those hours for work on another day, then I recommend trying that.

For instance, if you close up shop five hours earlier than usual on Halloween, can you have people come in a half hour earlier for the next two weeks? (This is in a situation where people are literally getting paid by the hour, because you wouldn't want their income to suffer from leaving after lunch on Halloween to be with their kids. Of course, if you can give people Halloween afternoon off with pay, that's even better.)

The Overworked Businessperson scoffs at my suggestion of giving people prearranged paid time to enjoy Halloween, of course. But think about it this way: You will gain gratitude, happiness, loyalty, and increased longevity from teammates who know they have a good thing. If you can keep those people around, you save yourself the weeks of distraction, hassle, and decreased productivity that happen whenever there's staff turnover.

Giving people several hours off on Halloween will, in the end, save a great many hours for you and the multiple team members who would have to source, interview, hire, and train the replacements for the people who left your company because you didn't pay attention to their work-life integration. If the comp time model works, then you have sacrificed zero labor hours and saved untold labor hours for yourself and your team. Happy Halloween!

⊕

Executive Highlights: Work-Life Integration

This recap is extra direct, as a courtesy to people who are toggling between the commitments of their professional and personal lives. (Been there/am there.)

Snack-sized takeaway: *Respect people's time.* Structure your work interactions in a way that allows and encourages people to enjoy personal lives. This doesn't mean letting folks exploit your benevolence. This means being strategic about shepherding the team's morale and goodwill, which will translate directly into their increased productivity and commitment.

Business benefit: People work so much harder for you when they know they've got a good thing going in the humane culture and organized environment you intentionally foster.

Sustainable strategy: Stop emailing, texting, and calling colleagues between the hours of 9 p.m. and 9 a.m., except in cases of literal emergencies. (Make this "quiet window" longer if possible.) Let people know that they won't hear from you during those hours. This will make you a more focused and effective human the next day and will improve others' headspace as well.

Seriously, try this at home: Lower your standards. That is to say, stop driving yourself to mental and physical exhaustion by trying to achieve perfection in all things (whether it's obsessively formatting the paragraph spacing of a casual email or folding all the laundry before you go to sleep at night. Again, the window to my psyche is opening). Figure out when your ruthless quest for perfection is unwarranted and therefore needlessly draining. And, crucially, model behavior for your team to show them that, with discernment, there are times when it's healthy, efficient, effective, and humane to let good enough be good enough.

Even if you're not the boss yet: Say no sometimes: no to taking on an extra work project even if you'd like to be nice, no to an unrealistic deadline even if you're a people-pleaser, no to volunteering for committees and attending events even if you're being heavily guilt-tripped by someone in your orbit. Radically accept that just because you *can* do a thing doesn't mean you *should.* Free up your time and energy to excel at what's necessary in your work life and personal life.

To lead with work-life integration, you'll have to expand your tolerance for the discomfort of *letting your team members (and yourself) prioritize personal lives as well as work lives.* It might not feel natural at first, especially if you've been trained in dysfunctional environments. But the team's commitment will increase because of it. And you might find yourself enjoying a little more balance too.

But wait, there's more: Now that we're getting into the fully adult territory of being honest about our needs as human beings, it's time for us to grow up even more and look at the uncomfortable necessity that can make or break a team of human beings: accountability. Don't panic—this is achievable for even the most squirrelly among us. Read on....

CHAPTER 8

ACCOUNTABILITY PROMPTS CHANGE

"I f—ked up. I'm sorry."

*—Me, to a member of my team who I had
offended with a thoughtless comment*

I was recently on a committee that's looking for a new pastor for the Presbyterian church I belong to. (The above quote is not related to this anecdote!) As with most church activities, this was a volunteer effort, and all of us have busy lives. So our work had been languishing by the wayside until one of my good friends at church, with grandmotherly kindness, looked me in the eye and asked how the search committee's progress was coming along, because she was concerned that we were not only stalled but losing ground.

I had to admit to her that we were probably not going to hit our deadline of submitting a written report to the church's leadership group on Tuesday of that week. After that conversation, though, I realized there was no reason we couldn't get the report done by Tuesday if we all focused our efforts. With this concrete goal and request, I was able to rally the other members of the committee; working together, we completed our report on time.

The firm gaze of a church matriarch is not the only way to galvanize a team (though I assure you it is effective). What was actually at work in the above story was the power of executive coach Birgit Zacher Hanson's four *W*'s: *Who will do what by when, and why.* "Who" was the committee, "what" was the report we were supposed to submit by ("when") Tuesday night, and "why" was because that report was the necessary next step in the recruitment process for the permanent pastor that our church very much needs. This story is also one example of how accountability prompts change—namely, with clarity, specificity, and deliverables on an agreed-upon timeline.

When she was a performance enhancement coach for the New York Yankees, Zacher Hanson of Heads-Up Performance noticed how baseball coaches would instruct players how to correct themselves—for instance, "You swung too fast on that pitch. Lean back in your batting stance." And then the batter would usually get in their own head and overcorrect, which produced the opposite outcome (another swing and a miss) from what the coach and the player wanted.

One of the reasons the Yankees hired Zacher Hanson and her partner Dr. Tom Hanson was to help coaches coach differently and allow players to assess their own results and use a process of self-correction rather than directives from the coach. She built on this experience when she worked with Veterans Affairs. There, she guided leaders to coach rather than tell their team members what to do; she taught leaders to urge team members to connect deeply to what they care about, focus on what they want, and trust themselves to come up with a workable strategy that would produce desired, sustainable outcomes.

So instead of saying, "Do what I tell you," the leader asks, "What's your assessment of the situation, and what do *you* think is the best way to improve on this going forward?" Then the leader asks the team member they are coaching to make a commitment to do that thing on a specific timeline in order to achieve an agreed-upon goal. (This management tactic is the subject of the Hansons' excellent book, *Who Will Do What by When?*)

If the team member in this dialogue can't commit to the requested task or deadline, then they can make a counteroffer—for example, "I can't provide that information on Friday, but on Friday I can give you an answer as to when I *can* provide the information," or "I think the information you're requesting won't actually solve the problem at hand. Can you give me more context for your request so that we can figure out together what is actually needed to solve this problem?" The process empowers all participants to get specific about expectations, reasoning, deliverables, and timelines.

And if, after a dialogue, the answer becomes a firm "No, I can't or won't do the thing you're asking," then the next step is either a conversation to identify and resolve what is causing that "no" or an acceptance that this person is declining the request. This understanding, at the very least, gives you the clarity to direct your efforts elsewhere, instead of letting your energy seep away in an endless wait for unanswered emails, unresolved questions, unattended responsibilities, and unfinished tasks.

Here's the critical takeaway:

> **Every time you ask someone
> to do something, get their
> agreement for that commitment
> through specifying who will
> do what by when, and why.**

"If you haven't gotten a commitment from the other person yet, then you technically don't have a right to complain yet," Zacher Hanson said.

For your part, you should make commitments to your team and honor every commitment you make. You will be amazed at how much more you get done this way. You also could be possibly humbled by the existing disconnects this method reveals—even if it's just the disconnect of throwing a spotlight on the fact that you've been afraid to ask for a timeline on a time-sensitive project. "Honoring a commitment is different from keeping it," Zacher Hanson pointed out. "We can't keep all of our commitments, but we can always honor them by following through, renegotiating before the deadline, or [offering] an apology and a new commitment after a deadline was missed."

I vividly remember experiencing this sequence of events when I was younger in my career as a TV writer and had much less Zen in my heart. At the time, I had just joined the staff of a TV show that had an established team dynamic, and I was writing my first solo episode. We were in danger of falling behind schedule because it was almost time for us to send a completed script to production for the first day of prep.

(Sidebar about network TV production: If you don't have a completed script ready for production on the first day of prep, the Directors Guild of America [DGA] will fine your show several thousand dollars for not honoring the union agreement to give the episode's director the basic tools [in other words, the script] to do their job on day one of the [usually] seven days they're given to prepare for directing the episode.)

So, the clock was ticking down to getting a DGA fine and throwing production into disarray, and my supervisor had sent my completed draft to our boss the showrunner, who would have to read and sign off on it. That was a necessary step before we could deliver it to the production team, who would then begin the fast-paced process of prepping the episode (scouting locations, building new sets, auditioning and casting guest stars, choosing costumes for all the actors, and finding consensus on and budget for a mountain of other logistical and creative details) in order to film it seven business days later.

But even with the real-world constraints closing in, other team members didn't want to "rush" our boss. The long-standing process in place was to send the boss a script and then wait on pins and needles for a reply; like all showrunners, ours had a schedule that was packed all day long, and they happened to be traveling that week as well, so it was difficult to predict when they would find time for any given draft sitting in their email's inbox. And my stress grew.

As the deadline became imminent, I had a coaching session with Zacher Hanson, and she advised me to email my boss to ask if they could read and respond to the script by the following afternoon so that we could keep the process moving and send the script to production on time. My boss promptly and cordially emailed me back: Sure, they'd read the script while on the plane to Los Angeles. And they did, and we kept the show moving on time and on budget. It's all because I respectfully used Zacher Hanson's accountability tool of "who will do what by when, and why?"

If you had a knee-jerk reaction of "but I ask people to commit to a timeline, and they refuse to answer me! Or they say yes to a timeline, and then they don't deliver on the timeline! What am I supposed to do then?" then you are not alone. This is an incredibly common experience in the workplace.

As is still my go-to practice, I asked Zacher Hanson for coaching about the above. Before she answered the question of "what am I supposed to do when people don't honor the commitments they made?" she gave me two caveats.

First: "We want to be able to count on the commitments that people make and the integrity with which they make them. These tools are not silver bullets; they don't fix character flaws. When someone is just rebelling and refusing to give a commitment, you have to say, 'What are you dealing with here?'"

Second: "You have to ground your assessments in reality. As a leader, you're not entitled to get commitments just because you're a leader. It might be that what you're asking for is not actually in the person's job description. If it's not in their job description, you can't hold people accountable to things they never committed to in the first place." (For instance, asking an administrative assistant to start picking up your dry cleaning.) "'No' is also a commitment," she noted.

But let's say you have made a request that is within the team member's job description, and they agreed. Basic example: Your supervisor committed to giving the team a daily lunch break at 1 p.m. However, several days have gone by, and you keep breaking for lunch anywhere between 1:10 p.m. and 1:40 p.m., with no discussion of how this doesn't match with what you agreed on. Here are your next steps:

1. *Declare a breakdown.* That might sound daunting, especially if you are making this declaration to your boss. But this is not personal, Zacher Hanson said. "It's just a statement when things that would normally flow are

interrupted. In business, in order to keep psychological safety, it's best to bring attention to a breakdown, because that's something we can fix. If you make it about a person, they're going to get defensive, and then it derails."

When you declare a breakdown, you acknowledge that you didn't do the thing you agreed you were going to do. (For example: "I want to check my understanding about an agreement I heard us make the other day… we were going to take a daily lunch break at one p.m., is that correct? If yes…well, we haven't been doing that, so we have a breakdown in that commitment not being honored. Are we still committed to the one p.m. lunch break, and if so, what can we do to correct that?")

2. *Get curious* about what stopped them from succeeding in the commitment the first time. Ask neutral, fact-finding questions to help figure out a more effective path forward.

3. Have an *impact conversation* where you explain the ripple effect of the breakdown. Tell the team member why folks were counting on this commitment, and provide contextual reasons (for instance, when we didn't go on our lunch break at 1 p.m., this other person had to cover the phones, and then she was late for her next obligation).

"This impact conversation is something that is usually missing," Zacher Hanson said. "Hold up a mirror and say, 'This is what happened when the commitment wasn't honored.' Do this in a kind way so that people know you're not mad at them, but this was the impact, and in the future, we need [them] to renegotiate the commitment before the deadline and take responsibility for [their] actions.

"People don't necessarily want to see and feel the impact of their actions or lack of follow-through, but we need them to see the bigger picture," Zacher Hanson said. "You can explain the impact with softening statements—'I'm not calling you out; I'm just trying to help you understand the mechanics of how we honor commitments here'—so that you preserve psychological safety. 'I still respect you just as much as I did before, but now I'm training you in this operating system.' Get out of judgment—don't just use it like a hammer or make it personal and wound or shame people—in order for 'who will do what by when, and why' to be a system that people can use and spread. Try to depersonalize it because everyone can learn a system and a language. If [they] refuse to learn the system, then that gets evaluated in the team member's performance review."

4. *Get a new commitment* from the other party about who will do what by when, and why. That's the whole goal of the "declaring a breakdown" conversation. You want to figure out *what commitment will get the desired outcome.*

   In this way, the ownership of the responsibility (for getting something done and getting desired results) is given to the people whose job it is to do it. This is a change from team members saying to the manager, "You tell me what to do," which keeps the monitoring of the process on the manager's plate.

Zacher Hanson summed it up like this: "Most managers tell people to do what by when, but then they don't *shift ownership of the completion* to the team member. The team member needs to accept responsibility for the outcome versus the manager saying,

'This needs to happen because I told you to do it,' then they wait, and if the outcome doesn't happen, the manager is upset." She advocates for changing the entire system, so that the tasks that team members commit to become theirs to own the management of and accountability for.

As for the somewhat knottier problem of people who refuse to even answer you when you request a timeline, Zacher Hanson had tough-love advice: "When people don't give you a commitment, call attention to it: 'I understand it might not be comfortable for you to tell me by when you will be done thinking about this, but I need to be able to put it on my calendar to move the process forward to the outcome we both want. If you need to renegotiate your projected timeline along the way, we can do that.'

"To ask for a commitment in that way is not about creating urgency, it's about creating clarity. It's better to close the loop with a small commitment like, 'I will work on this script in two months,' rather than leaving the loop wide open by saying, 'Whenever I am done with cleaning out my garage, I will get back to writing this script.' However, there might just be people who don't want to commit. And then you have to think, are these my ideal clients or colleagues or supervisor?

"If you inherited a team with this resistance to making commitments, then you declare a breakdown: 'This team is not willing to commit to the vision.' When people say, 'I'm not willing to commit to anything,' then you say, 'Take a look at your job description, and if you are actually refusing to do your job, then as a leader I have the authority to write you up for not doing your job and enforce consequences as appropriate from there.'" But this is the last resort. The hope is to train people about the language and mechanics of a commitment-based operating system up front, to avoid punitive conversations like this.

So part of accountability is *making direct requests and actually letting people know what you expect and need, and continuing that conversation until you get a commitment from the other person*—or until you make it clear what the consequences are when people leave the loop open, or when they outright refuse to meet the requirements of their job description. This can be uncomfortable, which maybe is part of why so many of us avoid it.

Sometimes, though, accountability is taught in a way that is impossible to avoid. While the below case study is an extreme example, it created remarkable cohesion and a sense of every person being directly responsible for and accountable to the rest of the team. This bond has lasted across decades and continents in life-and-death situations, and everyone who was a part of it still remembers where it was indelibly solidified: on a rugby field.

Case Study: The Rugby Team at West Point

Brian Anthony is a West Point graduate as well as a former Green Beret and army ranger who served multiple tours of duty in the Middle East. I was very curious about the team-building practices of a world so far from my own. (If you haven't noticed yet, I'm intentionally including case studies from as wide a variety of environments as possible, because the tenets of leading with kindness apply to every possible workplace, and in surprising ways.) With this chapter in mind, I asked Anthony how military training instills a sense of accountability among colleagues who have to rely on each other as individuals and as a group.

"It's very rigorous and very demanding," he said. "They're going to break you down and erase you and then build you back up with a common identity. They want to show you that it's not about you, because there are very few instances where you can do it on your own. It's not like having a star in the NBA, where sometimes you just give that person the ball." He said that one of the main themes of his training at West Point was to show how much more can be achieved through collective effort than through individual effort.

"There's also a character-building element that involves sacrifice for other people," he added. "In the military, the stakes are so much higher because you could die, or worse, your negligence could result in the death of somebody else. I also think, taking a step back, you're building love for an organization—a unit, a group, the Marine Corps—they make you love an institution. You've become part of something bigger than yourself. There's camaraderie for the group and for the person next to you—and you carry that pride and love with you. You want to talk about accountability—if you love somebody or something, you are accountable to it, and they are accountable to you."

When I asked him to share specifics beyond what I'd seen in movies that show military training, Anthony immediately thought of his time on the rugby team at West Point. "Our coach was an old-school West Point grad. At the end of practice, we would do conditioning, and all of this was under the pretext of getting you ready to go to war. We'd do 'suicide drills' when we were tired, because that's when the conditioning is most effective." He described this as a kind of running drill where you had to run to every line on the field and then back to your starting point, progressively working your way all the way down the field. Then, you'd work your way all the way back. If you did it right, you'd do that once. If you didn't… you'd end up crossing the field many, many times.

And then there was this one night when something extraordinary happened.

"The coach would kick a rugby ball out into the field and call out one player's name. That player had to chase the ball down, and they'd have to try to make a kick from wherever they got the ball. If they missed the kick and didn't score, then the whole team would have to do another suicide drill." The best kicker was called first, then the next best, then the next best after that, and everyone kept missing the kick.

Every time another player missed their kick, the entire team had to sprint through another suicide drill. The forwards (beefy players similar to linemen in football) almost never kick. And they started grumbling. So, the coach started calling their names to kick. But they missed their kicks too. Suicide drills resulted for the whole team each time.

Anthony remembered the experience like it was yesterday. "The sun was going down, the stadium lights were coming on, our legs were burning, we were missing dinner at this point. Eventually, even the grumbling stopped. Just dead silence and grunting and running. We went through the whole team, ran the whole field thirty times, all the way down the roster until the team captain came up again, and he made the kick. And the coach just walked away without comment." After that, the exhausted teammates were finally allowed to leave the field.

Over twenty-five years later, when that same rugby team gathered at a memorial service for their coach, *everyone* talked about that night of the missed kicks and the sprinting drills.

"It was the first story that came up," Anthony said, with strong affection in his voice. "Incidentally, that experience brought out not just accountability for the team members to each other but love in a lot of ways. Love for each other, love for the game, love—in the long term, if not that night!—for our coach."

I asked Anthony: Did the coach ever talk to you and your teammates about that night? Like, did he give you all a pep talk or a hug for working so hard? The answer was an unequivocal *no*: "He was not a huggy guy."

"It's gonna ruin the story," Anthony laughed, "but I went to visit him a few years before he passed away, and I asked him about that night, and he said, 'I wanted to send you guys home from practice, but I couldn't. I was so pissed. I just wanted you guys to make a f--king kick.'" But Anthony then added that this coach— Lt. Col. (Ret.) Mike Mahan—had decided not to pursue further promotion in his military career because Mahan determined that staying on as the rugby coach at West Point was how he could best train and build leaders of character for the army and the country.

Mahan's training worked, too. After continuing to play on the rugby team throughout his time at West Point, Anthony graduated in the spring of 2001. The vast majority of his rugby team was deployed to Iraq and Afghanistan, where they served in combat and continually relied on their sense of accountability to each other.

It's an unusual example, true. But the takeaway for me and hopefully for you is this: When every member on the team feels and exercises a personal responsibility for what happens to the entire group, then the team you've built together can withstand profound trials.

⊕

An equally important and even more uncomfortable aspect of accountability is that it requires difficult conversations when things go wrong. Ideally, you have those conversations with radical empathy, and you acknowledge realities and take actions to create change—whether that change is a negative consequence like benching a bully or a positive evolution like making a storyline more culturally authentic. The efficacy of and reception to those kinds of accountability measures are greatly impacted by the *way* you have the conversations surrounding them.

Sometimes, however, the conversation itself is the only pathway available for a situation that can't be easily remedied or changed. In another world far from my own—medicine—these difficult conversations happen every day.

May Pian-Smith, MD, served as the quality and safety clinical director for anesthesiology at Mass General Brigham, a sixteen-member institution that is the largest private employer in Massachusetts. I asked her how doctors handle it when they need to talk to patients after something goes wrong—from things as simple as a crowded waiting room to as complex as a troubling diagnosis.

"People want to hear you say you're sorry," she said. She wasn't talking about issues of liability or fault; she simply meant the act of expressing compassion from one human to another after something bad has happened. She also said it's important to discern what state the other person is in—anger, bargaining, acceptance?—in order to give them space and empathetically meet them where they are.

If a doctor is talking to a patient about an evolving case, she said they'll use language like, "'This is what we know so far. I promise we're going to keep reviewing the situation, and as we learn more, we'll share it.'" She explained further: "I use the word 'promise' because it's a human word. People don't want to be left out on a limb—they want to know there's going to be some kind of resolution and understanding at the end of this."

One of the things that struck me about Pian-Smith's approach was that it was very validating of the patient's experience. It was centered around *compassionate respect for the emotional life of the other person.* That aspect of the difficult conversation is important when you take accountability for a mistake with a respectful apology.

Elements of a respectful apology:

1. Take ownership of what happened.
2. Apologize for the specific impact on the other person.
3. Refrain from explaining away or justifying your actions (in other words, leave out the "but" and the part that attempts to minimize what you did or why you did it).
4. Stop talking and let the other person respond.
5. Allow uncomfortable silence to be part of this process. Don't rush this step.

Let's say you're on a conference call with some executive colleagues, and you express frustration about something happening with a group of people at your workplace. Then you belatedly realize that someone in that group of people was actually on that same conference call, muted, and taking notes while you spoke poorly of the group. Now you've stepped in it and offended a coworker (which also makes your preexisting problem worse). The easy thing to do would be to pretend it never happened or to decide this coworker should just tough it out and accept your (harshly phrased) assessment. But we're not here for the easy way out. So as a leader, you choose to apologize, in person, as soon as possible.

Here's where the above accountability tools come into play. You resist the temptation to justify your comments with an excuse like, "I was under a lot of stress at that moment, and this frustrating situation has been going on for a long time despite my best efforts, so I was just venting." And you resist telling your coworker how they're supposed to feel with a direction like "I hope you didn't take it personally when I said that thing on the conference call." And you resist trying to mitigate your misstep with a disclaimer like, "You know I didn't really mean it, right?" or "I was talking about those other people, not you."

Instead, you dig deeper and follow the five steps above, like so: "I f--ked up. I'm sorry. I was wrong to make a disrespectful comment on that phone call. What I said was hurtful, and I apologize for how it impacted you."

Beat. Beat. Beat.

(In a TV script, that's how we write a screen direction to indicate that several seconds of silence follow a line of dialogue.)

After that silence, more silence from you follows, while you let the other person respond. Is this uncomfortable? You bet. Is this discomfort worth it, while you hold yourself accountable as a means to rebuilding your colleague's trust? Absolutely. And in this example, my coworker accepted my apology, and they also acknowledged me for being so forthcoming and accountable in how I had expressed my remorse to them.

(A footnote to this anecdote, and a painful and humbling lesson I learned so that you don't have to make the mistake I made: *Don't vent to other colleagues.* It never pays off. I recommend writing in a journal or talking to a therapist instead. Quite seriously. Anytime you vent to a colleague about mutual acquaintances or peers, part of your colleague's brain will be thinking, "What do they say about *me* when I'm not around?" They might also take the liberty of repeating what you said to the very people you do not want to hear it.)

Just as with effective team building, an effective apology begins with holding yourself accountable as a leader—from an administrative perspective, certainly, but also from a moral perspective. If you don't set the tone and enforce the course correction for what behavior is and is not acceptable in your organization, people cannot fully trust or respect you. But when you demonstrate that you deserve that trust and respect, and when you show that you hold yourself to exact same high standards that you ask of those around you, then people will go above and beyond for you in loyalty, performance, and results.

So, quick regroup on how to create and sustain accountability in yourself and others:

1. Use Birgit Zacher Hanson's approach for getting commitments: Find agreement on "who will do what by when, and why."
2. When there's a breakdown in a commitment, declare the breakdown, be curious about why it happened, have an impact conversation, and get a new commitment.
3. When you make a mistake, own it, and respectfully apologize as soon as possible.

And...this is all well and good when you're in a leadership position and/or have some measure of control over the interactions in question. But what about when you need to hold other people accountable for their toxic behavior towards you or your colleagues? And what happens when the behavior is coming from people in power? This can be challenging, but it's incredibly important—not just for you, but for others around you who might be negatively affected by a colleague's or boss's conduct.

I will first say that I've been surprised to discover how much benefit there is to the larger group (whether it's your internal team or your work community as a whole) when you simply acknowledge that someone has acted harmfully. By "acknowledge," I mean literally naming the actions at all, even separate from trying to remedy them. I learned this when I went on the record for Maureen Ryan's book *Burn It Down: Power, Complicity, and a Call for Change in Hollywood.*

In that book, Ryan's investigative journalism detailed the dysfunctional and hostile work environments behind the scenes of a large number of TV shows. So many people who read that book, myself included, felt a great sense of relief that we were no longer being gaslit by people telling us (via silence, obfuscation, or outright denial of the facts) that these bad things had never happened. There's power in simply saying out loud: *This happened, and it was wrong.*

But after you've stated out loud that the toxic behavior (bullying, harassment, discrimination, verbal abuse, and so on) has happened, what's the best way to hold people accountable for it?

I asked Ryan for her thoughts on this, and she replied: "I wouldn't tell someone to talk to someone who had harmed them or was toxic if they couldn't do it safely. But if it won't harm your mental or physical health or your financial future to talk to them, you could find out if this person even knows that they upset you or hurt you or damaged your relationship. If none of those things seem like the right option or a person gets an unsatisfactory response when that conversation happens, the first step is to find out if there's a community that can come into play. Communities can move mountains.

"After the 'Me Too' movement, what really changed is that people now understand that if something negative or damaging happened, it's entirely possible that they're not the only person who experienced that. In a way that doesn't put people at risk, sound people out. See if there are other trusted people around. That accomplishes two things: The person asking might feel validated. Also, you're beginning to form a group, and people can put their information together. Multiple heads are better than one. When you talk to other people, a plan for accountability can be built. You can find out if there's more damage being done."

Realizing the power of groups in holding perpetrators accountable, Ryan joined the board of Callisto, a nonprofit that offers an online reporting portal about sexual assault. If there are matches to other reports in the Callisto system, survivors can (with consent) be put in touch with each other. "It's really powerful to be validated and to know that you're not alone," said Ryan. "And the plan that you might want to execute when you're not alone might be really different from what you might want to do on your own."

She continued: "The very first misconduct story I did after 'Me Too' broke open—I had nineteen sources for that story about allegations regarding Andrew Kreisberg. None of the sources were named. It was really important to me that people did not have to jeopardize their mental health or their careers but could still get accountability for what had happened. A lot of those people were assistants, script coordinators, junior writers, support staff. A number of people, many of them support staffers, got accountability for a major producer with an overall deal at a studio. That was possible. We don't always notch wins, but they are possible because people who were told for a long time that they had no power came together and they did have power.

"The huge part of any oppressive system is to tell you that you have no autonomy and no power. In every industry, people are told, if you go against the power players, your life is over, your career is over, you're done. I would certainly never say that this is without risk. Of course there's risk. But all of these people taking a leap together was so paradigm shifting. And what I saw was people who still had fear, but they said, 'Whatever status I have, I'm going to put that to work in service of this.' It helps people's mental health and their healing and cathartic journey, and it can help them career wise." Ryan cited how successful many of her interview subjects have continued to be, after going on the record with her. "This is why I get very annoyed when people with very high status and less risk don't do more to protect people and shield people," she added.

Ryan's potential ire is its own form of accountability—her effectiveness as an investigative journalist proves it—but that's not what prompts me to say she's right. I agree with her because it's up to the rest of us to protect and shield those who are the most vulnerable in workplace situations. Psychological, emotional, and verbal abuse happens every day due to imbalances of power between leaders and their team members, and among members of teams as well. Wanting to stop that kind of abuse and toxicity was why I wrote this book. It's also why I really hope you'll use these strategies to do right by the people around you and prevent harm in your own workplace. It will bring me to our next topic—safety—right after this handy recap.

Executive Highlights: Accountability

This recap is particularly important if you avoided this chapter because you knowingly or unknowingly resist being accountable to others, but you have a gnawing feeling in your soul that you could do better at owning up to your actions and choices.

Snack-sized takeaway: Accountability may feel daunting because it requires openness and a measure of humility. But you can reframe both those things as a display of fearlessness and integrity, because if your actions are consistently above reproach, you never have anything to hide or be ashamed of. Holding yourself to the highest standard of accountability for your actions and choices will engender the respect and trust of the people around you.

Business benefit: When you set an example of accountability, you make it safe for others to do so as well. When the team knows that everyone is safely accountable for their actions and choices, the work improves, the culture gets healthier, and people can fully trust each other. All of those things pay off in the team's results, longevity, and effectiveness.

Sustainable strategy: On a monthly or biweekly basis, ask your colleagues for feedback about your job performance. This includes colleagues who report to you. Their feedback doesn't have to be detailed or lengthy. The goal is to normalize the practice of offering and receiving constructive comments, so that everyone can course correct as needed. As a leader, provide similar check-ins for the people you supervise. These check-ins serve as both a timely pressure valve for concerns and a regular forum for positive reinforcement.

Seriously, try this at home: When you need to apologize for something, truthfully acknowledge the impact you had on the other person, but don't explain the circumstances that led to your actions, and don't justify your choices in a mitigating light. Example: Instead of saying, "Sorry I'm late, but there was so much traffic, and I had to do this other thing before I could get in my car," say, "I'm sorry I disrespected your time by making you wait for me, and I apologize for making you sit here alone." And then stop talking.

Even if you're not the boss yet: Be respectfully candid when a lack of accountability from a colleague (including a supervisor) is impeding your ability to work towards a shared goal. Then make a specific and neutral request for accountability to help you get to the desired outcome. An example for this kind of conversation with (let's say) a supervisor who has stalled your workflow due to their radio silence: "I'm really excited about making our project a success. I'm requesting your feedback on the current phase so I can move forward with improving it for you. By tomorrow, can you provide the timeline for when you'll share further guidance?"

To lead with accountability, you'll have to expand your tolerance for the discomfort of *owning up to your mistakes*. It's humbling, but when you hold yourself to the highest standards and take responsibility for your missteps as well as your achievements, you'll find that people respect you more for it, and you might be surprised at others' capacity to extend you grace.

But wait, there's more: Now that you have some tools to foster accountability in yourselves and others, you can take comfort in the fact that it becomes easier with practice. This is great news, because it feeds into one of the most important responsibilities of all: the safety of your team. This will also bring you greater success. Read on....

CHAPTER 9

SAFETY IS ESSENTIAL

"The 'dream economy' preys on
the dreams of people who come to
Hollywood [and] are then told, 'If you
want to break into this industry, you
have to do whatever it takes,' [which]
essentially includes abuse of all kinds."

—*Liz Hsiao Lan Alper, writer-producer
and founder of Pay Up Hollywood*

This chapter goes far beyond the borders of the entertainment industry, but the entertainment industry is where my journey with this topic starts. On February 20, 2014, I was in the Atlanta parking lot of *The Vampire Diaries* production offices when I saw crew members sobbing, holding each other. Whispered voices relayed that there had been an accident on a film set in nearby Savannah, and someone had died.

The specifics gradually emerged. The crew of the independent film *Midnight Rider* had been instructed to "steal a shot" on a bridge over a river, where they had put a hospital bed and actor William Hurt on train tracks to film a scripted dream sequence.

But the director and producers had chosen not to get permission for this from the railroad company, and no one had been posted along the active tracks to give any warning to the crew if a train approached—which one suddenly did at nearly sixty miles an hour, forcing crewmembers to run towards the oncoming train in order to reach the narrow walkway that was the only exit from the bridge. A twenty-seven-year-old assistant camerawoman named Sarah Jones was one of those crewmembers, and she was struck by the train and killed.

Sarah had been a beloved member of *The Vampire Diaries* crew in prior years, and the outpouring of grief and rage over her senseless death had a profound impact on the entertainment community. With support from *The Vampire Diaries* team, I helped Sarah's parents start the Sarah Jones Film Foundation in her memory, with a mission to foster awareness and accountability for safety on set.

More than ten years later, our work is far from done. As I've risen through the TV ranks, I've been able to make safety a priority for the productions I lead. It's not just about physical safety, though of course that's the first necessity, but also safe surroundings for mental health and emotional well-being. By normalizing ongoing communication about safety-related concerns, and by quickly and appropriately responding to those concerns, you *show your team members that you are valuing and protecting them as human beings.*

That strategy seems incredibly basic as I write it out, but I'm constantly surprised and dismayed to hear about workplaces where employees' essential needs are willfully disregarded. For instance, I've known people who had to work in a corporate building with moldy air vents, where respiratory illnesses became common among the office staff. And I know multiple cautionary tales from workplaces that emotionally bullied from the top down, which caused lasting trauma and quick attrition especially in the youngest employees, who were frequently people with intersectional identities. This means psychological safety is also a factor in efforts towards including diverse voices for improved business results. The leaders in these situations seem uncaring or at best resigned to decreased efficiency and cratering morale.

Maybe those leaders don't see the cause and effect, but no matter what field you're in, ensuring the safety of your team is a crucial element of earning and deserving their trust—and without that trust, they cannot perform at anything approaching 100 percent. The nonaltruistic way to look at this is that safety will absolutely move the productivity and profitability needles in the right direction. The way I prefer to look at this, though, is that creating a safe environment is the fundamentally decent thing to do, which is a worthy goal in and of itself.

"How much of my environment can I *create*?" you might ask. More than you might imagine. Turns out you can intentionally generate psychological safety through techniques developed by hospital chaplains who, during the COVID-19 pandemic, forged into unknown territory: conveying empathy and providing solace to patients who they were no longer able to see in person.

Case Study: The Hospital Chaplains Who Created Safety Over the Phone

Northside Hospital is an Atlanta-based system that operates trauma centers and clinics across Georgia. To learn about what happened there in the spring of 2020, I spoke with Reverend Amani Legagneur, Northside's system director of spiritual health and education. She's much more than a hospital chaplain—she also plays a part in shaping the well-being of every person in the Northside ecosystem.

Legagneur described the pandemic as "a time of great fear, of loss of orientation, of existential crisis, really." For safety reasons, before vaccines were readily available and when personal protective equipment supplies had to be carefully managed, hospitals worldwide often restricted the number of family members and other people going into patient rooms. Clinical staff who did not need to touch patients physically were challenged to provide support in new ways. Hospital chaplains normally provide "high-touch" care, in-person visits where compassion can be conveyed both verbally and through physical presence. Without the ability to make bedside visits, Legagneur and her staff had to find a new way to offer care to patients. They also had to marshal their resources—five full-time chaplains and eight student trainees serving about six hundred patients plus the entire hospital staff—to reach as many people as possible, around the clock, while also minimizing the risk of contagion for themselves and others. The question they faced as crisis responders was this: Is there a way to show, demonstrate, and communicate care even though we can't always be physically present?

The chaplains were relieved to find an answer in old-fashioned phone calls. First, Legagneur and her spiritual health education team trained the chaplains to invite people to lean in by using their tone of voice very carefully. "Over the phone, it was warm-heartedness and communicating that warm-heartedness—pausing a lot to listen," that was so successful, she said. They had patients who had difficulty talking because COVID-19 is a respiratory illness, so conversational techniques had to become very specific: "Slowing down a lot—to be aware not just with our ears but with our entire set of senses, to figure out where their area of need was—was our whole task."

She gave one of the most important pointers for having an empathetic phone conversation: "Remember to pause." For students who were talkative by nature or who kept talking anxiously because of the intense circumstances, she would tell them to actually count their sentences: "Say two sentences and then stop. And see how it feels to be in rhythm with another person. Almost like a dance. Say two sentences, stop, and allow them to have some space." After you've given the other person that space, only then do you start to come up with your next response.

To teach the skill of finding that rhythm of communication, Legagneur's team had to do a lot of training through role-playing. "It was very interesting because there's a whole generation that doesn't talk on the phone," she said. She had to remind her students, and anyone who was a millennial or younger, that they could trust themselves to have the same conversation on a phone that they would have with someone in person: "Imagine that you're in the room with them. What does your body feel right now? Are you checking in to make sure the other person understands what you're saying? Are you conveying hospitality from the very start of the conversation, and bringing that energy into your voice?

"Over the phone, you might say, 'I'm smiling right now,' or 'Wow, that makes me feel like I need to take a deep breath with you,' so you have an embodied experience with the other person. 'If you don't hear me talking right now, it's because I'm taking a minute to process what you just said.' So, you're *narrating* what you're experiencing."

Legagneur also strengthened the chaplains' ability to nurture the patients on the other end of these calls. She did this by having the chaplains visualize a time when they had felt really connected with someone even though they weren't in the same room and talk about elements of what had helped them feel connected to that person. Often, those elements were loving affection, a profound mutual respect, an alignment of values, or a sense of being deeply listened to. So, the coaching was this: "Think about a time when you were talking to somebody who wasn't physically with you, but you felt their presence in the room with you, felt that they were truly there with you. That's what we were trying to accomplish. By remembering what it felt like to experience those nurturing, connected conversations from the past, they were able to enact that more successfully with others."

As for training the chaplains to convey empathy via Zoom, Legagneur said they helped people learn to show their heartfelt care through eye contact. She had chaplains practice smiling with their whole face, despite wearing masks. "Trust your eyes to translate the intention that's in your heart, mind, and soul—that positive regard you have for the other person."

Whether on Zoom or on the phone, the key component of creating psychological safety in conversation is the authenticity of your concern, communicated with compassion and listening skills. Those listening skills include using responding techniques like paraphrasing and summarizing or asking for details with minimal prompts, so that people know they're being listened to. "Look for feeling words," Legagneur advised. "'This has been a hard day.' 'Hard day?' That invites people further into the feeling, and then they'll bring you more into their experience."

The tele-chaplaincy that Legagneur taught was centered around making sure the person on the other end of the call felt heard and witnessed. "Sometimes we can't alleviate suffering, but we can bear witness to it. Our patients said that they felt more relief and comfort from having had those encounters. And we were just grateful every time it worked—it felt like a bridge, and people really needed a bridge at that time."

"People were so isolated, especially when they didn't have their family members at their bedside…they felt so alone and sad," she remembered. "So, we would hear about their families, their physical condition, and what was on their hearts. If there was any rupture at all within their family, they'd want to talk about reconciliation. They'd want to talk about why a benevolent God would allow them to suffer. They would talk about social needs—'I don't know how I'm going to feed my children; I have to get out of here. Am I going to die? I'm not ready for this.' When people figure out that we're not going to run from those questions, and we're not going to ignore them or try to inauthentically resolve them with platitudes or bromides, they open up—and beautiful things can happen, even if they're difficult things."

To connect the dots in this case study from a completely reductive business perspective, you can apply the empathetic listening and conversational skills used by hospital chaplains to build rapport with colleagues, clients, and even adversaries. In this way, *creating psychological safety will lead you to productive outcomes.* But also, restoring a sense of safety is a basic first step within a humane response to overwhelming circumstances. And the humane response is what this book is all about.

⊕

Returning us to the everyday workplace: You can and should create a culture that has safety as its foundation. That's because:

> **Safety creates harmony,
> which enhances
> productivity, which
> increases (your) success.**

Hopefully you have the basics already in place: an environment with adequate light, heat, shelter, water, restrooms, and so on (I'm thinking back to some of the nighttime forest-location shoots I've been on), so that people can do their best work in a physically secure setting. Beyond that, I urge you to give your team members a confidential and welcoming mechanism for speaking up whenever they notice something that doesn't feel safe to them—whether it's an outdoor staircase that's become slippery in the rain, or an unmet need in physical accommodations.

You should also encourage people to come forward when they feel the workplace challenging their mental health and emotional well-being, but naturally those issues can be more difficult for people to disclose. I've found that the best way to generate a functional team dynamic is to be very clear from the get-go about expectations for professional behavior. This means setting standards for what is acceptable and being at the forefront of maintaining healthy boundaries among team members.

And, as much as I'd love to say that all humans can intuit what professional, healthy behavior means (and then adhere to those standards of behavior), I've found it extremely beneficial to actually *tell people what the standards are.* Like, spell them out so there can be zero doubt. It might feel slightly awkward to state things like, "In this workplace we don't comment on body types" or "On this team we don't belittle each other's work," but you should only have to say them once. Won't it set your mind a little more at ease when you're in the office, knowing that those are the norms that everyone has agreed on prior to walking in the door?

As a leader, you have the opportunity and responsibility to set those norms. Through those norms, you'll establish the tone and culture for your workplace. In the world of television production, we can find ourselves opening up new workplaces every few years as shows come and go. With each new team of writers, actors, and crew members, you get to give some version of an opening-day speech where you bring them into your vision for the harmonious, efficient, and high-performing culture you're going to create together.

This doesn't have to be an actual speech—my go-to is a welcome email that I send all my new writers and department heads, telling them about the workplace culture I intend to foster. You can find my welcome letter to the *Nancy Drew* writers in Appendix I, and you'll see how I used it as the first building block in our compassionate and kindness-driven workplace. I'm a person who means what she says, and because I was willing to articulate my intentions, I set the tone for everyone else. You can do this exact thing too.

Articulation is actually the key. It doesn't have to take long to establish *workplace agreements* where all team members reach a stated (emphasis on stated) consensus about how they're going to treat each other and handle their daily tasks. This is not just for the sake of mutual respect and management efficiency, though both of those are important as well. The deepest benefit is that *healthy workplace agreements create safety for your team members.*

Ideally everyone on the team comes up with these agreements together and, after reaching mutual consensus, literally signs their name to the entire list of them. This might sound a little unusual, but just because it's unfamiliar to you doesn't mean it won't work like gangbusters. That's because:

Workplace agreements should manifest every tenet in this book: inclusion, kindness, trust, love, calm, transparency, work-life integration, accountability, safety, and service.

You can have an executive coach come in to guide the process of creating these initial workplace agreements, but you can also build the list as you would through any collaborative discussion. Workplace agreements include standard practices such as if person A has a concern with person B, they will talk to person B about their concern, instead of going behind person B's back and complaining to person C.

Or, workplace agreements could include the specific of "when we make requests of each other, we'll use the 'who will do what by when, and why' format." (See chapter 8 on accountability.)

Or, "When we receive emails from each other, we will at the very least reply with 'Received.'"

Or, "When we need a pause button in a conversation, we'll use an agreed-upon safe word."

Here's a small and innocuous example of this last agreement. When I start in a new workplace, I ask the team to agree on a "safe word" for when we need to call a time-out in a conversation. My current safe word is "birthday cake," and I realize that's two words, but I love birthday cake and exclaiming it aloud is generally not alarming to others. I'm easily embarrassed, so a discussion of bodily functions might cause me to pipe up with "Birthday cake!" in order to request a change of topic.

You'll be surprised how useful it is to have a prearranged ability to hit the pause button on a workplace conversation. Sometimes the practice is even useful (with or without a safe word) in a more casual setting, like lunchtime with colleagues. I once asked for a pause button when we were about to hear a granular description of a tragedy from the life of a coworker's friend. I asked my coworker not to proceed with the story because I didn't want the horrific details rattling around in my memory forever (I have one of those brains where I'm intrusively haunted by the vividly upsetting specifics of these kinds of stories for years and years afterwards). If my coworker had really needed to share the story and if everyone else at the table had given their consent to hear the story, I would have excused myself from the room, without judgment, for the purpose of maintaining a boundary around my own emotional well-being, thereby protecting my focus and productivity for the rest of the day.

Of course, in a workplace the issue can be much more complex than choosing your level of engagement with lunchtime conversations. In fact, the most problematic issues tend to come from the interactions where there is very little choice when it first happens. I'm talking about harassment and bullying.

Ugh. I know. These are unpleasant behaviors. But we don't have to be resigned to their existence. In fact, there are ways to proactively mitigate and even prevent them. And leading with kindness is all about being proactive.

⊕

If you're reading this book, you are probably aware of the general wisdom that devoting resources to basic training and providing oversight concerning how team members treat each other will save you money and time in the end, because you won't be paying for litigation and remedies resulting from workplace harassment claims.

Workplace harassment is a sprawling topic beyond the scope of this book, but the headline is that you, the leader, are responsible for what happens on your watch. So I urge you to refresh your memory on the specifics of your state and the federal law concerning what is not allowed in the workplace, as well as the consequences for breaking those laws.

Hopefully you're in a wonderfully nurturing and gentle environment, but just in case you're not, you might have noticed that harassment is more likely to occur when there are extreme power disparities within the work ecosystem, when the people who have the most power are also the least subject to oversight and accountability, and when those powerful people have unquestioned access to vulnerable people around them.

An example from my industry is when the star of a TV show is emotionally and verbally abusive to members of the crew and the writing staff, and everyone knows this is happening, but no one does anything about it because without that star actor, there is no TV show. Unfortunately, the entertainment industry's tendency to prioritize stars, budget, and timeline over the safety of others—and the underlying *myth* that brilliance requires toxicity—can lead to harm and harassment.

Often, the burden of reporting harassment and making formal claims falls on the people who have been harassed. Those folks may be reluctant to voice concerns due to (sometimes very valid) fears of retaliation. The people targeted by the harassment might also be experiencing job insecurity and additional stressors as part of marginalized groups, which makes it even more challenging for them to speak up. Other people who are aware of the harassment might also avoid getting involved for reasons ranging from simple discomfort to their own fear.

But when there's no consequence for people doing harmful things, the behavior becomes tolerated and normalized and might even be seen (especially by the perpetrators) as acceptable. The more normalized the behavior becomes, the more chance it has of escalating in intensity and frequency. The longer this cycle goes on, the harder it is to intervene and correct it.

But, whether you're the leader or not, it's possible to make an environment safer through *bystander intervention*.

The most effective way to break a cycle of harassment is by intervening on behalf of a vulnerable person as soon as possible. Meaning: If you're a bystander and you see that someone is being harassed, *you should intervene the first time you witness the behavior*. The goal is to prevent an escalation in the situation and to disrupt a pattern of behavior (which is likely affecting multiple targets) before it has a chance to spread.

Here's an overview of *the five D's of bystander intervention*, as explained to me by Tashmica Torok, founder of Aletheia Coaching and Consulting. When you see someone getting harassed, follow these steps:

1. *Direct.* Address the situation in the moment. Point out what's happening and name the harm in a safe and respectful manner. Ask a direct question (you don't even need to label what you witnessed as inappropriate), such

as "What do you mean by that? It sounds like you're saying that this person is less qualified to work on this project because of their gender. Am I understanding you correctly? Our code of conduct is clear: We do not humiliate people here."

2. *Distract.* Draw away attention (in extreme situations, this can be a literal distraction like intentionally knocking over a glass of water). The point is that you're stepping in to give the targeted person a break. You can also course correct a conversation in a way that isn't confrontational but instead educational. Ideally, you'll give people better language in a way that doesn't punish someone or condemn them for saying a certain thing. The point is not just to tell people that they're wrong but to change the culture. In other words, help people learn how to improve their behavior.

3. *Delegate.* Find someone to assist you with the situation. Maybe this means calling a supervisor. Maybe it means asking a colleague to come into the interaction while you go find the supervisor. But, as in CPR training, don't just ask vaguely, "Can someone call 911?" Instead, point to a specific person and say, "Will *you* please call 911?" or in this case, "Will *you* please come hang out here with this person, until I get back?"

4. *Delay.* This can simply mean slowing a conversation down so that other parties have time to join the interaction and respond. But if it's not safe to intervene, and if the above strategies are not helping or are escalating the problem, sometimes you can put a pin in a situation and tell people you need to do some other task at hand right now, but you can return to this conversation later. That

said, after you assess the safety of the situation in the moment, don't use discomfort and conflict avoidance as excuses to enable a harasser through inaction.

5. *Document.* Keep a record in writing about the time and place of an incident, what happened, what actions were taken, how the impacted person felt, and what the results were. Also check in with the person who was targeted, multiple times if needed, and make a note of how those conversations go. If you email these records to yourself, you'll have a time stamp of the documentation and a backup in the cloud.

After these steps, if the harassing behavior doesn't change, you need to make a report. Your workplace policy (and state and federal employment laws) has to be administered equitably even if the perpetrator is powerful, charming, a movie star, and so on. That's the only way for your team to feel truly safe.

So, quick regroup on providing a safe workplace and working dynamic:

1. Be intentional about protecting your team on a physical, mental, and emotional level.
2. Articulate what the standards of behavior are, and hold everyone to those standards, which includes enforcing consequences for not meeting those standards.
3. Establish workplace agreements that specify how team members treat each other.
4. If you witness harassment, use the five *D*'s of bystander intervention: direct, distract, delegate, delay, and document.

⊕

And what about changing the culture that allows harassment in the first place? How do we change the power disparity, lack of oversight, and unquestioned access to vulnerable groups that result in conditions where harassment persists? I asked Torok about this, and her answers were illuminating.

1. Power disparity: This can look like unequal pay or a gap in privilege between an inner circle and the wider community. In Hollywood terms, it could be how a production caters to a movie star's every wish while the same production overworks and fires crew members without hesitation.

    To start to bridge this divide, Torok suggested: "Acknowledge the power disparity in the room, and look at who has the power. Have a conversation about practices and agreements about how we plan to use the power in the room and how we won't use it. And then actually do those things. Take the risk to change the paradigm by creating policies to protect and give autonomy to people who are the most vulnerable."

2. Low oversight: Abuse gets worse when impacted parties are in isolation, so we need to shift the dynamics that allow harm to occur. One effective approach is to flatten the hierarchy of a workplace by creating shared leadership positions. This way, power doesn't get concentrated in the hands of just one person who gets to act however they please.

    Our egos don't always want to share leadership, especially if we've been on a long journey to become the leader and if we genuinely believe we know what's best for the team. To be clear, I'm not saying that experience and wisdom should be sacrificed in a flattened hierarchy. I'm saying that when you have more than one safe person in the room for an interaction and more than one safe person on an email chain or a text thread, you create a safer environment because someone else will have a record of what happened. When there's visibility for the interactions of leaders and their team members, you allow for more protection from the community.

3. Unquestioned access: Often it's a charismatic, wealthy person in a position of power who is exempted from the expectations of the community. These people can do whatever they want because they're not held to the same standards as everyone else.

    Torok said that in cases of sexual abuse that are exposed after a long period of time, sometimes what you hear from the community (such as a university or a town) is some version of "we had thought the perpetrator was a lovely person who did great things for the community and that gave us the impression that we were safe, so we never imagined it was possible that this charming person was abusing people." In these instances, the person has groomed the entire community while targeting people who are vulnerable, less likely to be believed even if they do speak out, and don't have as much support from others.

The mitigating approach is to make it clear that nobody is exempt from the community and workplace agreements about the standards of behavior—not even people with money, privilege, and status. That's easier said than done, I know, but this is a book about difficult changes too.

If you just had a knee-jerk reaction of "but I'm not in a position to make sweeping culture change right now. And I can't speak up about safety issues or workplace harassment. I'll get labeled as a troublemaker and that'll hurt my chances of promotion/success/ my next job," then that is a totally human worry, and also I'm sorry to hear that you might be in a workplace that is not receptive to your needs—or that you might be in a situation where you think you'll be specifically punished for raising concerns.

The implied or real threat of that kind of retaliation is what employment law is meant to protect you against, but I understand that there can be a wide gap between what the law says versus what might be currently tolerated in your workplace. Even so, there are anonymous reporting mechanisms, and HR doesn't have to be the enemy; in my experience, those folks are actually very well trained, sensitive, discreet, and helpful.

However, if you don't believe that reaching out to your company's HR department will be fruitful, or if you're not in a job where there even is an HR department, there are other places where you can make your voice heard. As just one example, RAINN.org has multiple confidential and free online and phone options for reporting harassment and assault, twenty-four hours a day. This hotline is among many other such reporting mechanisms at both the national and state level, and I strongly encourage you to reach out to at least one of these places if you don't feel safe speaking to someone in your own work orbit.

I recognize that all of this is easier for me to discuss from the comfortable distance of my laptop than it is to take action in the field—particularly if you're the one being harassed or bullied. The isolation of that experience is one of the reasons it's so difficult to speak up about. That's why it's crucial to find allies (even via anonymous channels like RAINN.org) to help you seek recourse.

Meanwhile, if you're the ally in this situation and you're looking out for the welfare of someone else on your team, please persevere and know that you are doing the right thing—not just for the workplace you're in but for the human next to you. And that's also the point of this book.

Executive Highlights: Safety

Do not skip this recap. And if you were avoiding this chapter because it contains tough love, but you also want to avoid workplace lawsuits, then don't skip the chapter either.

Snack-sized takeaway: Safety is crucial. It isn't just about physical safety, though that's a basic starting point. You also need to take care of the mental health and emotional well-being of your team (ideally because you value being decent to others but at the very least in order to follow state and federal laws against harassment). Explicitly stated guardrails—physical and ethical—free up people to do their best work. Guardrails also prevent lawsuits.

Business benefit: When you create a physically safe environment, when you do not tolerate bullying or harassment, and when you treat everyone with calm professionalism (which includes transparently answering questions and addressing concerns about any workplace situation), people can work from a secure emotional and psychological place. People produce better and more consistent results when they're not in danger, freaked out, or demoralized.

Sustainable strategy: Provide your team with a clear reporting mechanism for harmful acts and situations. These reporting mechanisms vary from state to state, some are tailored to different industries and labor unions, and some are available at the national level. The fact that you've empowered your team with an anonymous hotline and/or website to bring concerns to will be a deterrent to unsafe behavior. Plus, you and your team should make use of this reporting mechanism in the event of concerns about unsafe working conditions.

Seriously, try this at home: For smaller matters (for instance, when a coworker's sense of humor makes you uncomfortable), establish a neutral sounding "safe word" to signal a time-out in conversation. Voicing a lighthearted safe word can give a coworker a gentle flag on the play before and/or after they cross a line.

Even if you're not the boss yet: Document all safety-related matters in time-stamped emails to yourself. This way you'll keep an accurate record of times, places, what happened, how you felt, what the impact was of the event, who you communicated with about it, what was conveyed in your communication, and what happened as a result. You can then refer to these records in case of an HR investigation or lawsuit, though hopefully neither of those will be needed.

To lead with safety, you'll have to expand your tolerance for the discomfort of *intervening when others are being targeted or impacted*. Speaking up about harassment or other unsafe working conditions might not be easy or popular, but if you don't do this, you're not a leader.

But wait, there's more: Now that you've gathered the rewards of planning for your team's physical, psychological, and emotional safety, let's bring all of this home with what I believe to be the most fulfilling and uplifting part of being a leader: service to something outside of yourself. Don't leave me now, Overworked Businessperson! Being of service will also make you more successful in your career and in your life. Read on....

CHAPTER 10

SERVICE IS TRANSFORMATIONAL

> "If I search among my memories for those whose taste is lasting, if I write the balance sheet of the moments that truly counted, I surely find those that no fortune could have bought me."
>
> —*Antoine de Saint-Exupéry*

> "I needed someplace to channel my outrage."
>
> —*Rachel Colwell, actress and Indigenous community advocate*

Maybe you didn't think the last chapter of this book would start with a quote about outrage. Those were Rachel Colwell's words about what spurred her social justice work, which we discussed when she was on my *Lead With Kindness* podcast. The context for that conversation was how she had become involved with community efforts to demand action from the Canadian government and the Catholic church following the discovery of hundreds of unmarked graves next to the Kamloops Indian Residential School.

Colwell is Ojibwe, and generations of First Nations families had been deeply scarred by the abusive and dehumanizing practice of forcibly putting Indigenous children into residential schools that were designed to strip them of their cultural identities. Thousands of children never returned to their homes, and those who did dealt with the effects of psychological trauma for the rest of their lives.

Like many other Indigenous people, Colwell responded to the news of the Kamloops graves with a renewed determination to be of service to her community. She now helps individuals get access to government services and is active in efforts to find healing and raise awareness for Indigenous issues.

I bring up Colwell's journey because it's worth pointing out that service can be a place to put our moral compasses to good use, and it can be a productive means to deal with concern and overwhelm and yes, outrage. But service is also a place to find purpose, exercise altruism, and forge community, and that's the focus of this chapter.

Before I get into the farther-reaching aspects of service to individuals, communities, and the world (I told you I was ambitious), let's look at the ways that service is of value in any business setting. Those ways might be different from what you expect.

The basic element of service, of course, is from your team to its clients. This becomes an important part of the work culture for your team, so it's crucial to put intentional effort into it. During the years when he helped manage multiple imaging centers, Harvey

Greenberg, MD, knew that patients would be anxious when they arrived for their MRI exams. So he instituted a practice of giving people warm chocolate chip cookies, because who doesn't relax when they smell chocolate chip cookies? The cookies were in a take-home bag with the imaging center's logo on it. The technicians and doctors benefited from this welcoming environment as well, and it reminded everyone of the shared humanity between medical professionals and the people they served.

You're probably also used to thinking of service in terms of how your team members help each other, and naturally in however they provide service to you. However, the startling proposition I'm going to make is that *you* need to be of service to your *team*.

"But they're supposed to serve *me!*" you complain. "I'm so busy. I have all the responsibility. I'm under so much pressure. Haven't I fought and scrapped and persisted to become a leader so that other people will do what I tell them to do? Am I not paying them to help *me*? What is this annoying suggestion that I have to *serve them?*"

Point of clarification: Being of service to your team is not the same as serving them. You certainly won't be waiting on them or coddling them. They might actually receive your service as slightly unsettling, because it may be outside of their comfort zones, and it may push them in directions they hadn't previously considered. Here are important examples of the kind of service I'm talking about (and you'll see that each will contribute to your success as well).

- *Mentor new team members. Onboard them individually and as a group in a way that articulates the culture you're creating and the skills they'll need to thrive.*

When I start up a writers' room, we spend several days building the team with mindfulness teaching, executive coaching, boot-camp workshops with department heads in production and post-production, and a public service outing where we volunteer at a nonprofit in the community. My investment of time and intentionality pays off richly in the bonded, trusting, and well-informed team dynamic that results.

- *Put team members into duos or small groups so that people who are newer to the job can get mentored by people who have been at it longer.*

  Make sure they have a structure in place for regular internal check-ins (weekly or biweekly usually works well). Touch base with all parties on at least a biweekly basis yourself, even if with just a brief email to make yourself available for questions and feedback. This practice allows the team's cohesiveness and training to progress with minimal time investment from you.

- *Help your team get access to career development resources in order to grow and deepen their knowledge of your field.*

  As part of my volunteer role as an elected member of the board of directors of the Writers Guild of America West, I cofounded and continue to help teach the annual Leadership Training Program for TV writers who are several years into their careers. Our curriculum teaches not just the skills to manage writers' rooms and production environments but also the best practices to design and lead workplaces centered around kindness, accountability, transparency, and other humane considerations. This is aimed at raising everyone's professional game and changing our workplace culture.

- *Respectfully exit a team member who is underperforming, so that the rest of your team isn't slowed down and picking up the slack.*

  When I say "respectfully exit," I mean with documented conversations about performance and expectations, along with as much consideration as you can give in terms of a severance package or two weeks' notice to give the team member time to transition out and train their replacement. I realize it's not always possible to include those things when you let someone go, but your compassion, and the manner of your parting, will have a significant impact not just on the person who's leaving but also on the rest of your team as they witness how *you* handle this departure.

- *For people who don't see this particular career path as their long-term life goal, help them find a road map out of their current position if they've outgrown their surroundings or if they're not the right fit.*

  Some management consulting jobs are structured with the full expectation that an analyst will leave the company after two very intense years of work—and in fact, the firm will help those people find their next jobs as the end of the two-year term approaches. Management consulting firms know this is a worthwhile trade-off in return for getting highly qualified and energetic people to work many, many, many hours a week while traveling like nomads from hotel room to hotel room. The takeaway: People see it as incredibly valuable when they get agency in their own futures. You can use this to your advantage in fostering the long-term health of your organization.

I can hear the objection from the back of the room: "Now you want me to encourage people to leave? I thought your thing was getting people to stay!" Yes, but think back to the goat pen and the adjacent goat rest area at the Atlanta zoo (from chapter 7 on work-life integration). We can all learn from the goats. Your team will be more committed, more focused, and more productive when their presence is a direct result of their *choice* and their *agency*.

Let's look at an example of this from a field that is itself service-oriented: immigration law.

Professor Huyen Pham teaches immigration law at Texas A&M University School of Law. She and her family fled Vietnam in 1975 after the fall of Saigon and came to the US as refugees. Pham and her family eventually ended up in New Orleans, and throughout her studies at Harvard College and Harvard Law School, she stayed intent on a career with a social justice impact. To this day, she finds meaning in working with people who are poor, stateless, and vulnerable in different ways.

With the students she teaches and trains, Pham is extremely mindful of how to set them up for longevity in the difficult field of immigration law. "Part of what our students need to learn is how to lose, because they're getting these cases that are really hard to win in today's legal and political environment. Burnout is also a risk if you're personally connected to the issues that you're defending," she said. Recently, she gave career advice to a former student who works for the federal government but who is disheartened by the government's manner of prosecuting immigration cases.

In her teaching, she makes it a point to expose her students to real legal settings, so they can see how the law operates and better hone their sense of how the law *should* operate. For example, she asks her students to visit the immigration court in Dallas to observe proceedings. She recalled how one student returned from his court visit visibly dismayed by the lack of fairness. The student saw that the court-assigned interpreter would only translate what the judge said directly to the immigrant and vice versa, but the interpreter did not translate what the lawyers or witnesses were saying in the courtroom related to the person's asylum case—leaving the person completely in the dark about how and why their fate was being decided. After witnessing this, Pham's student—who came from a conservative background—said, "That's nobody's idea of due process," meaning it was nobody's idea of the fair procedures that should drive the legal system.

Still, Pham said that those kinds of situations are helpful in broadening her students' experiences and helpful to her in keeping a space where students can talk across political divides and see the common humanity. It's difficult but meaningful work, and the immigration system desperately needs compassionate attorneys in the field. To help students find their best career fit and to understand how the other side operates in an adversarial legal system, Pham encourages her students to work in different legal settings during law school (government jobs, defense bar, and advocacy).

Similarly, you can be of service to your team in helping them find out what they're passionate about and where their greatest chance of longevity lies. You can help them be the best version of themselves so they can excel for you *or* so they can move on to another place where they're more fully aligned with what's important to them. And if they do leave, you've made room for a new person on your team who can be completely passionate about your work and better help you get to your goals as a result.

So, quick regroup on some of the ways that service can transform your work and workplace:

1. Service out in the world provides a way for us to make positive change.
2. Service from team members to each other generates deeper understanding and more lasting bonds.
3. Service from you to your team members can give them greater clarity of purpose and a discernment of whether their current job is right for them.

An encouraging human sidebar about service: When I talked to people from different faith traditions about how service fits into their lives and their heritage, everyone described it as being integral. Three examples:

- I asked Dr. Rama Amara to share his experiences concerning service from mentors to mentees while growing up Hindu in India. (These days, Dr. Amara is a core researcher at the Emory National Primate Research Center.) He said that in India, the mentor-mentee dynamic has a very personal feeling of responsibility. "In Hinduism, the relationships between mentors and mentees are very different because it brings in the responsibility…you're basically next to their parents. It is at that level. In fact, the parents trust the mentors with everything. So, the parents also treat the mentors at that level. In terms of kindness, the mentors always watch you and your moods—'You don't look happy. Is there something going on? Let's talk.' You sit down and understand if that individual is going through some kind of pain or problem, and try to intervene and help…In India, more people worry about you when you're not well, so you're not left alone. Sometimes you feel, 'There's too much intrusion into my privacy.' At the same time, when you really need help you have a lot of help."

- Rizwan Manji, an Ismaili Muslim actor, shared with me that service was an important part of his personal upbringing: "Since we were little kids, there would be community events where families would volunteer to support charitable organizations and advocacy for people in need." He also said that his faith tradition's orientation towards service extends into all aspects of his life. "We've been taught about balance between the spiritual and material aspect of life. There's not really a separation. It's the life that we exist in. It's part of your makeup. You don't set it aside when you're at work or at home…. There's no contradiction, no disconnect—you don't leave it all behind. The decisions I make, that's part of me being a human being, and I'm part of this community as well."

- Rabbi Sara Abrams described service in leadership as creating "the best kind of community through elevating, motivating, and being a role model for others." She also referenced the Jewish concept of *tikkun olam*, which is the collective action of putting a broken world back together, healing one fracture at a time. "Hopefully as we heal fractures, there's less *tikkun* for us to do, and we become more of a channel for the divine," she said. "Every person is here [to perform healing], mainly on themselves. In our healing and getting closer to the divine, we get to look at our own mistakes. When we do that, we become less judgmental of others as they go through their own process and unfolding."

These framings of service happen to resonate with me personally. But you don't have to come from a faith tradition or believe in a higher power to be able to do some good in the world. Let's talk about practical service through volunteering.

Don't skip past this part, Overworked Businessperson! If you just had a knee-jerk reaction of "volunteering? Are you kidding me? I cannot possibly sacrifice hours in my day to *help people for free,* because that will take away from the time I need to spend making money and telling people what to do and putting out fires and keeping the earth rotating on its axis," then you are not seeing the business benefits of how *volunteering will make your individual life better as well as raise the performance level of your team.*

Here's why I feel so strongly about service. Another formative part of my journey towards writing this book happened many years ago, during the long, long stretch of months I spent in the unemployed wilderness after not getting my contract renewed on an especially toxic television show. I had a lot of time for introspection, and I got extremely specific and intentional in making a list of goals for what I wanted to do in my next job. One of those goals was to incorporate public service into the life of the writing staff.

Soon after typing up that manifesto, I landed at *The Vampire Diaries*, and with my new bosses' blessing, I started spearheading public service opportunities for my colleagues. One mile down the street from our offices in Hollywood is an organization called My Friend's Place (MFP), which provides social services and transformative education for unhoused youth.

Having been impressed with MFP's work, I organized an outing for the writing staff to serve lunch to their teens one day. Learning about these young people's journeys and assembling modest meals for them gave us a way to be connected with and of service to our neighbors. It also provided valuable perspective on how fortunate we were in our own lives. The experience was bonding and fulfilling for us on every level, and I followed that up with similar outreach events on all the other shows I've worked on since.

To increase your team's sense of being present in their own lives and improve their connection to each other (both of which will make them better at their jobs, if you need extra incentive), I highly recommend taking them out of the office and putting them in a setting where they can truly be of service. (Do this during the work week if you can; please don't impinge on people's weekends if it's avoidable. That said, I recognize that not every environment has the flexibility for staff to leave the workplace, and the practice of volunteering is what's important here, no matter when you are able to schedule it.) Everyone I've ever done this with has found the experiences energizing, enjoyable, and inspiring.

There is no shortage of worthy causes, and I recommend inviting your team members' input to create service opportunities with organizations and initiatives that are meaningful to them. Ideally everyone should get a turn to suggest a service event, with group consensus of course. I also recommend engaging people in conversation about the volunteer work you're doing together—find out what their experiences have been in these realms, both good and bad. Asking for honest feedback will deepen everyone's relationship to their efforts.

Two pieces of advice to tailor your service efforts to your situation, from my own experience:

- For busy people: Ongoing mentorship is a great way to be of service in a way that you can more easily fit into your schedule. If you're mentoring someone who wants to follow your career path, even a monthly thirty-minute phone call while you're commuting to work is incredibly helpful. In these short and flexible pockets of time, you can be a valuable sounding board for someone who has questions and anxieties that you can provide useful insights on.

- For people who usually only contribute via their credit card (not that there's anything wrong with financial donations): Tangible goods can have more emotional resonance. When my younger son's Boy Scout troop had a pancake breakfast to raise money for wildfire relief, instead of Venmo-ing the funds to elementary schools whose libraries had been destroyed, we used the proceeds to buy physical books, added gift messages that said "Donated by BSA Troop 1, West LA," and then delivered the books to the schools. There's something about giving through old-fashioned, analog contact that can make the experience more memorable and profound for the giver.

No matter what the type of project, my goal in asking team members to be of service is to connect people with communities and causes larger than themselves—to broaden their horizons but also give them the actual satisfaction and rewards of volunteering. I truly believe that service to others is the only reliable way to raise one's resting state of happiness, whether through individual impact, social justice outreach, or gathering donations for nonprofits, all of which we did monthly as a team at *Nancy Drew* and *Tom Swift*.

> **Here's the enlightened self-interest argument for taking your team on a volunteer outing: The perspective shift helps people feel gratitude for the jobs they're in, and the mutual connection helps the team work more effectively together.**

Service to others is more than the secret sauce of healthy leadership. It's an essential part of living a meaningful life—which to me is the ultimate metric of true success.

Service links together and puts into action all the other tenets of this book. It includes disparate individuals, shows kindness, builds trust, concretizes love, generates calm, exhibits transparency, integrates life in the outside world with the work of the team, demonstrates accountability because you're giving back to larger communities, and promotes safe well-being because it provides a way for your team to compassionately and attentively engage with each other and those around them.

Best of all, it can be fun.

Case Study: Young Storytellers and the Writers' Room Of Nancy Drew

To bring this full circle, let's go back to the first workplace environment I designed: season one of *Nancy Drew*. We had been greenlit to production, and our first step was to assemble a writers' room (ten writers and six support staffers). In my past jobs, the writers' rooms I had been in had jumped into work on day one with very few, if any, get-to-know-you activities (on the first day in the writers' room of one brand-new show, we didn't even introduce ourselves around the table before the showrunner started talking about plot mechanics). As part of my kindness-driven culture, I set an intention to do it differently.

My welcome letter to the people joining our team specified that one of our very first activities would be a public service outing with Young Storytellers, which is a Los Angeles-based nonprofit that elevates the voices and narratives of underserved students. So, a few days into our first week in the room (after a day of team building with executive coach Birgit Zacher Hanson and before a mindfulness meditation workshop with Dr. Christiane Wolf), we met up at a public elementary school a few miles from our office building and were greeted in the gymnasium by the Young Storytellers staff and about twenty grade-schoolers. A few of our actors joined us for the event, and each student was partnered with an adult.

The workshop was very simple: The kids were asked to come up with a movie idea and then make a poster for it using colored markers. The facilitators presented the basics of story structure, guided the kids in articulating themes from their own lives, and helped them visualize the central elements of the movies they wanted to write about.

Lively discussions followed among the partners, who bounced around plot twists and action sequences and came up with the coolest posters possible. Along the way, we had a tasty lunch, and then each kid/adult pair went up to the stage (one of those tiny stages you perform the grade school play on) and giddily presented their movie idea, telling whimsical and exciting stories and explaining what the drawings on their posters were.

For the kids, it was a chance to be mentored by adults with jobs on a TV show. For the grown-ups, it was a chance to get back in touch with our childhood sense of wonder—the creative spark that had impelled us into pursuing our careers in the first place.

The other goal this service project achieved was that it was a way for our team to experience what it would be like to work on *Nancy Drew*. Our message to our audience, and my message to my team, was the same as what we gave to the kids with Young Storytellers: *You are valuable not in spite of who you are but* because *of who you are. We're making time to be present to receive and celebrate your experience of the world.*

And in that service project—just as we did in the four seasons of television writing, production, and audience reach that followed—we created something unique and wonderful together, and then we looked each other in the eye and said thank you. In short, we led with kindness.

This is why I chose that Saint-Exupéry quote for the start of this chapter, about those moments that truly counted that no fortune could have bought. I vividly remember being in that elementary school on a warm May morning, in a circle of excited kids making posters about the movies they could see in their heads, sharing their stories with delighted partners from our

Nancy Drew team. The sense of togetherness, hope, and possibility in the room—no fortune could have bought that. *Only service can get you that kind of joy.*

Service will restore your spirit and renew your sense of purpose, especially in difficult circumstances. And for anyone who feels like the world's circumstances are particularly difficult at this moment, I'll offer this encouragement.

Imagine that in your school gymnasium you'd built a beautiful village made of LEGOs, and then a tornado came through and scattered the pieces all over the gymnasium, all over the football field, under the stadium bleachers, and beyond. You can't possibly pick up all the LEGO pieces by yourself. There are too many pieces, and it's overwhelming to contemplate, because there are going to be pieces scattered everywhere for a really long time.

But what you *can* do is pick up the pieces you can reach. Lift up the people you *can* reach.

And trust that your example will inspire others to do the same.

Executive Highlights: Service

Hi again, Overworked Businessperson. You might have entirely skipped this chapter because it sounds other-oriented, but you should check out the recap because I promise it'll help you succeed. For everyone else, I really hope you share these practices and feel the lasting and empowering rewards of human connection.

Snack-sized takeaway: Service is not just for college applications. By connecting your team to the world around them and by being of service to your community—altruistically and effectively—you will elevate the team's concept of what is possible. Also, you'll actually make a difference in the world, which is what motivates anyone who's reading this book.

Business benefit: Moments of human connection are valuable and energizing and spread out positively to everything your team does. Giving people concrete results for their imagination, optimism, and efficacy in the world will reinforce those good habits at work.

Sustainable strategy: Organize monthly service projects for your team. This can be something with a very low bar to entry (such as collecting gently used clothing for a local charity—people often welcome the chance to declutter). I recommend choosing projects with a very manageable time commitment (for participants and organizers) and a high feel-good return, so that you can make service projects an integral part of the team's calendar and morale.

Seriously, try this at home: Hold the door open for a stranger, and then offer a smile when the person goes through the door that you're holding open. Not only will this improve the other person's day, but this simple act will also get you to slow down, come out of autopilot, and get in touch with the common humanity you share with those around you. This will reset your brain in a positive way.

Even if you're not the boss yet: Mentor someone who is newer to the career journey than you are—and mentorship can be as doable as an occasional ten-minute phone call to answer questions and provide perspective. Even if you are currently in your first job ever, you could be a mentor to a person who's still in school. There's also a bonus of enlightened self-interest: Taking the initiative to mentor someone else will improve your management skills, and it can become something you add to your résumé and talk about in future job interviews.

To lead with service, you'll have to expand your tolerance for the discomfort of *encouraging others to behave altruistically*. People may resist volunteering with you because they consider themselves too busy, too cool, too jaded, too shy, too any number of things. Your role as leader is to get those team members out of their comfort zones so that they can connect with a deeper part of themselves and have an impact on the world. The results will be worth it.

But wait, there's more: Like many narratives, this one has an end-credits scene. Read on for mine.

So where does all this talk of kindness leave us? You, me, and the Overworked Businessperson who's come along for the ride with us? (I see you, OB, and I'm glad you're still here!) I believe it leaves us with hope, and the capacity to put that hope into action.

Here's how I find hope for myself: I know these tenets of kindness are teachable, spreadable, and sustainable.

- *Teaching* the practice of kind leadership can happen one conversation at a time. I frequently have one-off mentoring phone calls with people who get introduced to me via mutual friends and other professional orbits. I spend a lot of time driving because I live in Los Angeles, and there's nothing that eases the pain of traffic on the 405 freeway like talking to a cool new person about how they can lift up other people. Every time I share a strategy that I've learned along the way and hear that it's making a difference in how the person on the other end of the call will practice leadership going forward, I am heartened and motivated to continue this work.

- My *Lead With Kindness* podcast is still *spreading* these ideas to anywhere that gets an internet connection, as I periodically find out from people (such as a high school classmate I hadn't heard from in many years) who tell me that their algorithm added my podcast to their phone's queue. The podcast is available on Spotify and Apple Podcasts, where you can also find transcripts for each episode. The whole reason I wrote this book was to get the word out about how leading with kindness is good for business (as well as being the right thing to do), so I hope each platform amplifies the other—and if these ideas speak to you, I hope you'll spread the word as well.

- As far as *sustaining* kindness, I am also very glad to report that intentional kindness is being installed in the educational planning for grade schools. In Los Angeles's Third Street Elementary School, the Making Caring Common program (developed by the School of Education at Harvard University) gives specific guidance and practical tools to create an uplifting, caring culture of kindness. With the support of this curriculum, bullying incidents noticeably dwindled, open communication intentionally increased, and student acts of kindness became the norm.

Let's hope that more elementary schools add kindness to the curriculum. I do think that what kids learn from other kids they carry with them for a lifetime. As a mom, one of my proudest moments was when I saw my son Jackson hanging out during recess with a couple of fellow students from his Saturday morning Chinese class. Jackson was fifteen at the time, and the two other boys were about eleven years old and eight years old. Jackson and the bouncy eight-year-old were playing basketball on the school playground, and the eleven-year-old—Ben, a shy, less spry boy—had retreated to the top of the slide, in a clear assumption that he would not be asked to play with the cool kids.

But when Jackson noticed Ben sitting up there alone, he called out and invited him to play. (Jackson has always had a gift for making others feel welcome.) So, Ben slid down the slide, and the three kids cheerfully played basketball together for the remainder of recess. Jackson didn't know that I was observing him from the sidewalk; there were no adults on the playground at that moment, either. So, when he modeled kindness for the younger kids, he didn't do so out of any expectation of praise or reward.

The best teaching, spreading, and sustaining of kindness is exactly how Jackson manifested it: not for external validation or self-serving results, but because it's the right thing to do, and because it lifts up the spirits and lives of everyone it reaches.

So as a starting point, as a call to action, as an encouragement for your childhood sense of possibility to come out and play, let me assure and promise you:

You can reach the people around you. You can have intentional conversations to understand them as they want to be understood. You can see the greatest version of them and bring that version out of them.

That's my hope for this book, and for everyone who encounters it—that these simple practices result in a lasting culture of genuine kindness in our relationships, our workplaces, our communities, and our world.

Thank you for being part of the kindness revolution. I can't wait to find out what we create together.

THE WELCOME EMAIL TO *NANCY DREW* WRITERS IN SEASON ONE

Hello Jesse! I wanted to let you know how thrilled we would be to have you join the Drew Crew. All of us were thoroughly impressed by the breadth and depth of your experiences as a person while also really responding to your voice as a writer. We truly hope you say yes to our offer, because while humbly acknowledging that we can't match the rates that others have paid you, what we *do* offer you is an awesome work environment and a lovely group of collaborators on a cinematic, emotional and complex show that we're incredibly proud of. Additional context for your consideration:

Start date is Tuesday, May 28th at our offices in Sherman Oaks. We're also planning a casual writers' screening/hangout plus lunch on Wed. May 22 (at the offices) to watch the pilot, download pertinent story thinking points, and introduce everyone to each other socially before having a nice lunch with whichever cast members are in town.

As an example of the work culture we're creating, here are the writer-bonding mornings that Noga and I have planned for our first few days in the room (the afternoons of these days will be spent blueskying)—

Tuesday, May 28th—morning session with workflow coach Birgit Zacher Hanson (her website is HeadsUpPerformance.com) to discuss how we'll approach the process of making this show, reach consensus on group agreements about how we collaborate with each other, and establish norms and protocols for creative interactions and decisions.

Wednesday, May 29th—community outreach with Young Storytellers from 9 AM to 2 PM at Valley Village Elementary School (Universal City area)—we're going to do a half-day workshop with Young Storytellers where our writers get paired up with 4th and 5th graders who will come up with movie ideas, poster designs and story pitches. (I'm a big believer in incorporating public service into our work life; this is my version of a Palm Springs retreat.) (YoungStorytellers.com)

Thursday, May 30th—morning workshop on mindfulness strategies and guided meditation—yes, you read that right. Dr. Christiane Wolf is a mindfulness coach who helps writers and other human beings manage their own anxiety and racing brains as a means to be more present, effective and engaged in their lives and work. Hopefully this will give us tools to re-center into the relaxed alertness that allows for ideas and words to flow more easily and more enjoyably. For her guided meditations:

https://soundcloud.com/insightla_meditation/sets/christiane-wolf-mbsr-guided-meditations

And here's another window into my brain: my notes to self about how to foster a writer- and family-friendly environment that also results in better work and a more fulfilling daily existence. These are my personal touchstones:

- QUIET by Susan Cain—how introverts thrive and contribute best when they're also given time to work by themselves and then come back to the group to share ideas, sometimes via email. If you want introverts to speak up in a group, it works best to say something like "In five minutes, I'll ask for questions," and then five minutes later the introverts will have really thoughtful questions prepared.

- The importance of creating an atmosphere of possibility. (Kenneth Branaugh quote on how he directs.)

- The goats at the Atlanta Zoo: In the goat petting zoo pen, kids were jumping and screaming and grooming goats with brushes, and the goats were totally calm, letting the kids go crazy around them. I asked the manager how she kept all the goats so calm. She answered, "See the adjacent paddock? There's a gate between this petting zoo and the goats' play area—"and she pointed to the next paddock, where several goats were sitting by themselves on bales of hay, staring into space, chilling out. "Anytime a goat doesn't feel like being in the petting zoo, it nudges its head against the gate, and we let it into the play area, no questions asked. So every goat here in the petting zoo wants to be here, *and knows it can leave anytime.*" Same principle applies to writers' rooms—let people know they can leave the room for school events and doctors' appointments and development mtgs; start on time, end on time, let people know dates and schedule and batting order from the get-go—in other words, remove unnecessary stress and uncertainty, and be extremely respectful of people's time and personal lives, which results in better morale and better work.

- Safety for Sarah: I'm on the Advisory Board for the Sarah Jones Film Foundation, which I helped create and expand in response to the *Midnight Rider* incident that caused Sarah Jones' death. In addition to the paramount importance of physical safety on set, we also hold ourselves to the highest standards of accountability in fostering a safe work environment for emotional, psychological and mental health.

- The first time the Patriots were in the Super Bowl, I was so excited to watch them come out. The other team was called off one by one as they ran onto the field—"Wide receiver, so and so! Running back, so and so!" Culminating with great fanfare in… "Quarterback, so and so!"—Then it was the Patriots' turn. And the announcer said: "Ladies and gentlemen… the New England Patriots!" And the WHOLE TEAM ran out onto the field together. And they won that game. By a field goal, mind you.

Saint-Exupéry quote: If you want to teach someone to become a great shipbuilder, don't teach them how to hammer a nail. Teach them to love the sea.

Jesse, I sincerely hope that you will give us the chance to increase your love of the sea. I believe that having you on our team will only increase our love of the sea as well. Thank you—warmly, Melinda

IF YOU LIKED THE BOOK, YOU'LL LOVE THE PODCAST

The unanimously positive response to my *Lead With Kindness* podcast convinced me to write this book; people are hungering for a positive culture change not just in Hollywood but also far beyond it. My podcast is available on Spotify and Apple Podcasts. At the latter, you can download PDF transcripts from the individual landing pages for each episode. You can also find the podcast via my Instagram: @ melindahsuLA.

(Bonus content on Instagram: You can access the free, one-hour recording of the Zoom meditation workshop I organized with Dr. Christiane Wolf in the wake of the LA wildfires to offer centering practices for our community.)

To give you an idea of the kinds of conversations the LWK podcast gets into, here's a sampling of the insights each episode contains. The episode titles, not coincidentally, match the chapters of this book. But while this book takes a deep dive into the strategy and how-to of each topic from a business perspective, the podcast episodes contain tales from the trenches and frank, emotional, and uplifting conversations with colleagues from my entertainment industry orbits.

Inclusion—Ruben Garcia, TV director, on how to foster inclusivity when joining a production team: "I may have some initial thoughts after reading the scene and seeing the location or locations…. And I'll ask the line producer, 'Well, what do you think about this? Does this work for us or should we do this?' And I've found a lot of times people are taken [aback] when they hear the question because they're probably not asked that very often. And so what I'm trying to do is I'm trying to give people skin in the game. And when they have skin in the game, and they feel like they can contribute to this director that they may have just met, you get them on your side, you get them on the team…. And now morale picks up and people feel like you're approachable, and all of a sudden I think you get performance out of crew and actors that you may not have gotten otherwise."

Kindness—Kennedy McMann, actress, on how to create an atmosphere of kindness on set as the star of a TV show: "The best thing that you can do for people is really set them up for success. How can I make sure that this person gives their best performance today? So when I get to work every day, if we have somebody new in, my top priority tends to be, how can I make this person feel really comfortable, feel a part of this, feel empowered to speak up for themselves?…If something goes wrong, if you're confused, if you need another take or if you don't know what's going on and you don't want to be the one to raise your hand and ask the whole room what's going on, just ask me. I can go and talk to somebody. I can ask for something for you. Filter it through me because I'm a person who can get that done. When someone's comfortable on set, [as] an actor, they're willing to take risks and to make choices, [after] making someone feel really comfortable, making them feel welcome, making them feel valued. And that's as simple as saying, 'Hey, I'm running to crafty [for a snack]. Do you want anything?'"

Trust—Andrea Thornton Bolden, TV writer-producer, on how to build trust with your team: "It's also how you begin. It's also the intention that you set forth with your writer's room or whatever, your crew, whatever the organizational structure is, being like, on day one, 'This is how we do things here.'…To say, 'Okay, in instances where there is harm, whether intended or not, this is how we will proceed. These are our rules, so that when we call each other in, we have a standard, we have a structure in place so that nobody's scared about what's going to happen.' It's like, no, no, no, you're not in danger. You're not going to be yelled at or castigated, this is how we call each other in, and then we decide to move forward as a team."

Love—Noga Landau, showrunner, on how to manifest love in a team dynamic: "One common thread that I noticed that I vowed not to carry forward on my own shows was this glorification of stress. I think that, in previous generations, even nowadays, TV writers have this thing where they're like, 'We have to be stressed. We have to wear it like a red badge of courage. Stress is a part of being a showrunner. Stress is a part of the day-to-day life.' As a result, there's all these practices that justify the proliferation of stress in an office. I literally saw it cause people to have health problems, mental breakdowns, arguments and inefficiencies every day that cost the show money…. Everything I've tried to do in my leadership is break the cycle, just because I was always told that it had to be this way, just because I was always told that, if you had a baby, you could only take a couple weeks off, or the job won't be there for you on the other side. If you have to go to a doctor, you can't go to the doctor…. You can't see a therapist. You can't leave the writer's room. You can't make a life because what if they suddenly need you? All these things, just because it was done before doesn't mean it needs to be done now, and we need to always be questioning that."

Calm—Andi Behring, TV director, explaining her professional mantra of "Slow down to speed up": "If you can slow down and be very distinctive about what the next step is, you actually go faster than if you try to rush people through. So that was learned by experience. I definitely originally would knee-jerk and say, 'Hey, come on, guys. We gotta get going.' But truth be told, the actors don't want to hear that, and they feel rushed and then their performance is compromised. So I'll tell them we have all the time in the world, even if we don't, so that they, again, feel safe and uplifted…. But I've found personally, if I need to really focus in and keep us moving forward, I do try to slow down and simplify, which seems counterintuitive but it actually really helps keep the train on the tracks. I've been on sets where the directors or the [assistant director] or the [director of photography] is just out of their minds. And it really trickles down to the rest of the crew and everybody's very stressed, and so there is a responsibility to set that tone all day that ['W]e're fine, we have a plan, we know what we're doing. We're going to get through this no matter what surprises come up.['] And that really did resonate through the crew."

Transparency—Akima A. Brown, founder and executive director of Reel Families for Change, on how to generate growth by using constructive feedback and *aggressive kindness*: "Sometimes kindness is when you're telling someone the truth in love…it's not a disrespectful space, but you're telling someone the truth, and you're holding them accountable, and you're bringing them to a place where they say, 'This is the area that I'm wanting to grow in.'…That's where the aggressive part comes into play is that you're not letting people run away from the growth process, the accountability process. You give them a safe space, you make them feel loved, you make them feel heard. You let them know, yes, you belong here, and if growth is your goal, you will get that goal, but you don't get to run away from it when it doesn't feel good. So that's aggressive kindness."

Work-Life Integration—Alex Taub, TV writer-producer, on the toxic environments he endured on his way up the ranks as a working parent before collaborating with me on *Nancy Drew*: "I remember sitting…up in some high-rise, and I'd hear ambulances coming. I'm like, 'Oh, I hope they're coming for me.' And at that point you're thinking, maybe I'm in the wrong business. But I remember one of the many, many things you did that I felt was very smart was if there was something you wanted me to write on a weekend or even on a day, and it's something that my nature would have me stretch out and do over the course of two or three days, you'd be like, 'Can we have that by lunch? I need that by four o'clock.' And then the rest of your day is clear. It's going to be much faster than you've done it [in the past], but it's very respectful of your time."

Accountability—Birgit Zacher Hanson, executive coach and coauthor of *Who Will Do What by When?*, on how to frame-shift when facing the difficult situation of holding someone else accountable for their actions: "I have a different lens as a coach because I do always want to bring it back to what can I actually personally control, right? Because if I empower myself with that question, instead of feeling like a victim, then I can take action, and that's what coaching is all about.… What meaning am I giving this? Am I feeling like a victim? Then I need to shift first before I can take action, because the more action we take from a victim place, the more divisive the situation becomes and the less we're going to actually problem-solve."

Safety—Rorelee Tio, stunt coordinator and stuntwoman, concerning keeping the set physically and mentally safe: "Things go a long way with a good conversation. You can always ask someone, 'Hey, are you okay? What's going on?' And that opens up the dialogue for discussion. And I know sometimes timing is everything. [When] we're in a time crunch…that's when people get really frazzled. But as a stunt coordinator, you really have to put your foot down in these situations to make sure that nobody gets hurt.… So I think…really from the top, if people are encouraged to speak when something is unsafe, then the crew feels empowered to also bring those up to the [assistant director], situations like that. And there's a lot of power in that."

Service—Ann D. Blanchard, Creative Artists Agency agent: "If people are just thrown together to do acts of service, the impact is subpar on the group as a whole. But if, as Ms. Hsu suggests, the team takes time before the service event to focus on their intention and their larger 'why' for caring as a team and working to act with kindness, then the larger impact is felt on both the team and in the world at large. Living with intention to transform with awareness as well as kindness is what the 'Lead with Kindness' movement is all about."

I hope you check out the podcast and resonate with the perspectives you'll find there. I also hope it improves your life and brings out the greatest version of you and everyone around you. That's my deepest intention with all of this. Thank you for joining me on the journey. Be well.

I deeply appreciate all of the Writers Guild members who shared their workplace experiences while we walked the 2023 picket lines together, as well as my many friends and colleagues in the business who have traded (and experienced) war stories with me through the years. Their fiery encouragement reminded me I wasn't alone and helped shape my determination to move this project forward.

The first step happened when my ever-innovative manager Jordan Cerf connected me with Elizabeth Baquet and the Ninth Planet Audio team to produce the *Lead With Kindness* podcast. My indomitable CAA agent Ann Blanchard was a guest on the podcast and told me afterwards, "Honey, this could be a book!" Ann then introduced me to Anthony Mattero at CAA in New York; he brought in editors Debra Englander and Caitlin Burdette with the Post Hill Press team. I'm incredibly grateful to all of these outstanding professionals for their support, insights, and guidance.

I'm also indebted to everyone I interviewed for the podcast and this book, both on the record and off. Our conversations were illuminating and uplifting and made me a better person.

And, I am so very thankful for my partner Harv and my sons Casey and Jackson. Their love, strength, and kindness are the center of who I am.